WELCOME TO
THE 90 DAY CHALLENGE...

How To Double Your Business In 90 Days Or Less:
*A proven 90 Day Action Plan that can DOUBLE
your business in the next 90 Days*

This book has been designed to be readable in half a day. Read
it in the morning, start work in the afternoon. BOOM!

WARNING: RESULTS GUARANTEED!

This book belongs to:

Name: ....

Address: ....

             ....

Phone #:   ....

Email: ....

If found, please return. As a reward:

Acknowledgements:

I am deeply grateful to my family for their consistent presence and love. This book would not have been possible without their support. You are the greatest gift that life has given me and I thank the universe each and every day for allowing me to experience life with you at my side.

Thank you also to the wonderful team of people I am fortunate enough to call both colleagues and friends. I'm blessed to be surrounded by genuinely good people who believe in me, and inspire me to keep giving my best. You know who you are.

PRAISE FOR SIMON STEPSYS

'Would you employ yourself based on the work you've done TODAY?' My friend and mentor Simon Stepsys asked me to think about that advice decades ago. I've never looked back!
Richard Mead, Entrepreneur

Simon is a true LEADER. I don't know anyone who has a more positive spirit and energy than him. He is very committed and ADDICTED to what he does. The most impressive thing is that he will always find time for you. People – including myself – love to be in his company because he shines out positive energy, and this energy helps to take people to another level. A positive mindset is key to success, and he's mastered it. Anything is impossible and he has proved it!
Vitalia Petra Kolesnikova, Business Owner

Simon's mentoring and guidance has transformed my business. By following his teachings, my eyes have been opened to a world of possibilities. My advice to anyone reading this book is to listen to what Simon is suggesting, and then take action.
John Robinson, Business Owner and Serial Entrepreneur

I sought Simon out in 2014 because of his expertise in the affiliate marketing space. Simon has elevated thousands of people across the globe. His specialty is team building through social proof and live events. He is a mind coach, and has contagious Attraction Marketing skills. His unselfish and always giving nature plants seeds into tomorrow's leaders. This man celebrates success at every level, and is proud of all who make progress. There isn't anyone that can compete with him when it comes to perception and promotion. His work ethic is second-to-none, which is why he gathers momentum and ultimate success. Since following him I have gone from failed and broke into the top 1% income bracket on the planet! I have made well over 7 figures and personally referred 9,919 new affiliates and counting. Thank you Simon for showing me what is possible. Because of your guidance and leadership, I am a better person in mind, heart and spirit. You are a leader who creates other leaders. Keep lifting, inspiring, educating and training!
Frank Calabro Jr, 7 Figure Blueprint Strategist

PUBLISHER'S NOTES

Simon Stepsys

Success International Limited

Simonstepsys.com

Published by Success International Limited

The author asserts the moral right to be the author of this work

Copyright © Simon Stepsys 2016

ISBN: 978-0-9933700-1-4 (hardback)

ISBN: 978-0-9933700-2-1 (paperback)

Printed and bound in Great Britain by CPI Books

TIPS FOR SUCCESS!

GET A MENTOR (it doesn't have to be me)

Be the 3 C's...

1. COACHABLE
2. COMMITTED
3. CONSISTENT

~ Simon Stepsys ~

**Would you like me to give you a
formula for success?**

It's quite simply really.
Double your rate of failure.

You're thinking of failure as the enemy
of success, but it isn't at all. You can be
discouraged by failure, or you can learn
from it.

So go ahead and make mistakes.
Make all you can. Because remember,
that's where you'll find success.

On the far side of failure.

This book has been written by someone who has produced millions of dollars in sales, not someone who just hopes to make it. If you follow this guidance, then there is absolutely no reason why you can't explode your business and income to another level.

I started with nothing; I used to sweep the street for a living. And now I'm a millionaire living the life of my dreams. This book shares how I did that, and how you can too.

I'm going to be sharing with you what I do each and every day to grow and develop my business. It's what I teach, and it's what I train. Why? Because it really works.

If you get this book in the hands of your organisation, your business will ABSOLUTELY be taken to another level. And as you begin to complete this workbook, you'll see and understand why.

Be EXCITED, be INSPIRED, because your income is about to go up in a MASSIVE way.

Congratulations and thank you for buying this book

In the pages that follow I am going to be sharing with you the secrets of my success in a simple and easy-to-implement 90 Day Challenge. You will learn the tools and techniques that have enabled me to achieve true financial freedom. The catch? You've got to reach out and take action in at least 3 to 5 ways each and every day for the next 90 days, or this will not work. I truly wish I'd had something as easy to follow as this book when I was starting out in business; however, I worked it out, and now I'm in a position to be able to share my knowledge with you.

**Follow the advice.
It really works!!**

Foreword by the author

This book is the coming together of decades of experience and I've written it with you, the reader, in mind at every stage. When I was starting out in business, a book like this would have been gold dust to me. Many people who want to build a business or start up on their own have little or no structure to their marketing plan – well, here is your structure and here is your inspiration.

What qualifies me to write this book?

First and foremost, I've been following my mentor's advice (as well as my own advice) for the last 30 years!

I started my working life brushing the streets for a living, and was introduced to Direct Sales over 30 years ago. I was online in 1995, making a full-time income by 1997. In two and a half years I've made over 30 million dollars in Direct Sales, team group sales of well over 250,000 million dollars, personally sponsoring over 5000 direct referrals into just one of my businesses.

I helped to build a sales organisation of over 300,000 members, creating multiple six and seven figure income earners at the same time.

So if I can do it, you can do it too.

As you read, I want you to feel inspired, confident, and powerful.

I want you to know that anything is possible: that you can live the life of your dreams. You can achieve success. You can get what you want.

BELIEVE THIS TO BE TRUE!

Getting what you want all starts with knowing what you want. Following that, you'll need the right mindset, and then you'll need to take MASSIVE and consistent action. This book is going to coach you through each of those stages. It is essentially an interactive workbook, and you'll realise the power of it when you begin to take action yourself.

I feel so fortunate that I am now in a position to be able to share what I've learned over my long career in marketing with you, the reader. Follow the advice in this book: I am living testament to the fact that it works.

And the best thing about it? It's so simple. There are over 100 Marketing Tips included. You are simply going to choose between three and five of these each day, and repeat for 90 Days. That's it. Do it for 90 Days and watch your business EXPLODE!

I wish you every success. Be the best and keep being **AWESOME!**

Your friend and mentor,
Simon Stepsys

CONTENTS

Your Commitment

Here is where you make the commitment to get SERIOUS about your intent to follow the advice and guidance contained within this book for a minimum of 90 Days.

Complete the following IF AND ONLY IF you are absolutely committed to taking action for the next 90 Days. If you hesitate to sign for whatever reason, I would urge you to seriously question what's holding you back. Ask yourself, 'If not now, when?'

"I _____ (print name) 100% commit to following the advice and guidance contained within this book for a minimum of 90 consecutive days from _____ (insert date)

Signed

_____

Congratulations: you have just taken the first step to DOUBLING YOUR BUSINESS, and therefore your income!

ACTION

Is the foundational key to all

SUCCESS

~ Pablo Picasso ~

INTRODUCTION
An Overview of The 90 Day Challenge

When you are in the KNOWING,
things manifest FASTER
~ Simon Stepsys ~

Welcome, and thanks for buying my book. You won't regret it.

How do I know you won't regret buying my book? Well, because I know that what I am about to share with you works. I know because I've been following my own advice not just for 90 Days, but for the last 30 years! That's right – for the last 30 years I've been taking action each and every day, and the results speak for themselves. In my career to date, I have successfully built teams and organisations all over the world.

I'm only asking you to follow my advice for 90 Days. But my guess is that once you start to see the INCREDIBLE results, you'll want to continue into the next 90 days, and the 90 after that. I'm going to be giving you a choice of 100+ actions, and you are going to select three to five of these and perform them daily. You might want to repeat the same three to five actions for the whole 90 Days, but my advice would be to mix and match them for maximum benefit.

> *THE SECRET OF SUCCESS:*
> *STOP WISHING, START DOING!*

As you read, you may be thinking, 'This is all a bit straightforward, I know all of this'. Well, you may know it, but you aren't doing it. My advice is simple for a reason, and I'll outline in Chapter 1 precisely why I've made the decision to keep things that way. It's simple to do but also simple not to do.

Just choose your three to five actions, do them consistently, and keep recording your progress in the back of this book. Then watch your business EXPLODE!

People think that in order to be successful you need to have money to invest; however it doesn't cost anything to be committed, driven and enthusiastic. You need to get your mindset right. In business, as in life, the mindset you bring to what you do is EVERYTHING. And so in Chapter 2 you will find a quick-start guide to preparing your mindset for The 90 Day Challenge.

If for any reason you begin this process but don't get to the end of the 90 days, you need to seriously look at why you're in business. Chapter 3 will help you to discover your 'Why' and set your business goals accordingly. It all starts with your 'Why' – why are you doing this, and also, why AREN'T you doing it? You need a reason, a driver, to push you forwards and I aim to help

> *NEVER GIVE UP JUST BECAUSE OF*
> *WHAT SOMEONE SAID. USE THAT AS*
> *MOTIVATION TO PUSH HARDER!*
>
> *~ Zig Ziglar ~*

you discover this, whether it be true financial freedom, a more comfortable life, to enjoy luxury or simply to free yourself from debt. Whatever your reason, it has to be big enough to drive you each day to take those three to five actions.

Once we've explored the importance of simplicity, worked on your mindset and established your 'Why', we'll move on to some practical preparation that you will need to do before implementing The 90 Day Challenge. This is all covered in Chapter 4.

We then move straight to The 90 Day Challenge in Chapter 5. Remember that initially, you may try a few things that may not work for you straight away, but the bottom line is that in business there isn't always instant success. You have to work. For some, this has meant 15-hour days before hitting the big time. Now I'm not saying it will be the same for you, but you need to be prepared to do what it takes. Remember: it's all about the mindset.

In Chapter 6, I've provided you with an Action Tracker to record your progress on. All I ask is that you follow the challenge for 90

Days, even if at the start you think it isn't working or you question the results. I assure you, if you do what I outline, it will work.

Remember this: if you don't take risks, if you don't take action, you will always work for someone who does.

Wishing you every success in all you do.

MAKE MONEY —
NOT EXCUSES!!

YOU WILL ATTRACT EVERYTHING THAT YOU REQUIRE. IF IT'S MONEY YOU NEED YOU WILL ATTRACT IT.
IF IT'S PEOPLE YOU NEED YOU'LL ATTRACT THEM.

YOU'VE GOT TO PAY ATTENTION TO WHAT YOU'RE ATTRACTED TO, BECAUSE AS YOU HOLD IMAGES OF WHAT YOU WANT, YOU'RE GOING TO BE ATTRACTED TO THINGS AND THEY'RE GOING TO BE ATTRACTED TO YOU.

BUT IT LITERALLY MOVES INTO PHYSICAL REALITY WITH AND THROUGH YOU. AND IT DOES THAT BY LAW.

~ BOB PROCTOR ~

Chapter 1

THE IMPORTANCE OF SIMPLICITY

Never overlook the power of simplicity

~ Robin S. Sharma ~

THE IMPORTANCE OF SIMPLICITY

CHAPTER
01

There's so much information out there – it's easy to be overwhelmed. That's why I've designed this book with simplicity in mind.

When I share with people how staggeringly easy it is to double their business so quickly with The 90 Day Challenge, I can almost hear their minds ticking over.

How can this be possible? they think. *There must be a catch,* they think.

Because it sounds too good to be true. However, it is true. And I am evidence of this truth.

As a race, we think that if something is complicated, if it is difficult to understand, then that justifies the rewards.

*THINK MASSIVE, DREAM MASSIVE,
BELIEVE MASSIVE, ACT MASSIVE AND
THE RESULTS WILL BE MASSIVE!*

But who said it has to be that way? Who said that something straightforward can't reap HUGE rewards? In our modern world, we often confuse simplicity with laziness; however that's far from the truth. Here are some truths that I've learned about the importance of simplicity:

 Simplicity doesn't mean compromising on quality
Focusing on what is most important and doing that well is not a compromise, but instead an exercise in getting really clear.

Doing a few things well builds trust. And trust builds business.

 Simplicity doesn't mean no effort
I'm not suggesting that a simple plan means no work. In fact it's quite the reverse: my plan only works if you do. It's simple because it can be replicated by anyone in business, almost anywhere in the world.

The 90 Day Challenge is so straightforward and easy to follow, you'll wonder why you didn't think of it yourself!

WHAT YOU THINK ABOUT YOU BRING ABOUT!

~ Lisa Nichols ~

Simplicity can help you to relax
And we all want more of that, right?

Once you begin to implement The 90 Day Challenge,
you can rest assured in the knowledge that you will
be growing your business in a way that is both proven
and effective. This means you can become much more
relaxed and free to plan, dream big and enjoy life!

 Simplicity can transform you
When you are free from the burdens of complexity and
the demands of so many different things and people, you
can begin to focus on what is truly important to you and
live the life of your dreams.

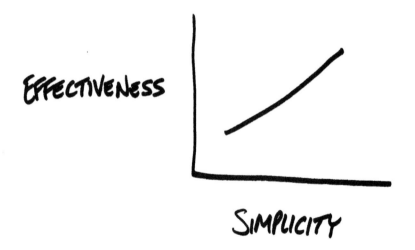

Now you know why I've kept things simple. Next, let's get you into a POSITIVE mindset ready for The 90 Day Challenge!

ONE WORD SEPARATES WINNERS FROM FAILURES:

CONSISTENCY

Chapter 2

GET YOUR
MINDSET RIGHT

✔

If you are going to doubt
something –
DOUBT YOUR LIMITS!

~ Don Ward ~

 **GET YOUR MINDSET RIGHT**

CHAPTER
02

The truth is this: you can achieve anything you want in life. You were born a winner, just like everyone else, and the only thing that stands in the way of success is your mindset. You're reading this book for a start, and so you're already a winner – you're already someone who has an interest in or dedication to improving him or herself.

Changing your mindset from negative to positive is a lifelong commitment; something you work on each and every day. I'm going to be sharing with you some very simple steps that can get you started today. Right away.

Because if you're anything like me, once you've made up your mind to do something, you want to get going immediately. This guidance will serve you well as you read through the rest of the book.

Before you read on, I want you to believe and know that you are a winner, that you can achieve your dreams. With the right mindset, you can follow your dreams and passions and you won't let anyone or anything hold you back. I want you to feel good about yourself and your life.

Mindset is everything in life. How you approach every moment of every day will determine the outcome of your actions. Do you approach life with joy, attention and enthusiasm? Or do you approach your tasks and responsibilities with negativity and resentment? When we put our all into the present moment and do the little things right, the bigger picture takes care of itself.

But to do this, to approach life in this way, you need to work hard on yourself, harder than you ever have before. And trust me: it's worth it. By following the guidance here, you'll be amazed at how your life will change for the better – and not only your life, but the lives of the people around you too.

People just love positive people. Actually, let me rephrase that: *most* people love positive people; some of course love negative people! It's all about conditioning, and it can be easy to judge people who are negative, but just remember that they may have been born into negativity and may not know any different. Rather than judge and speak badly of them, you can choose to help.

Remember that in the same way, we are all conditioned in our belief about life. For instance, we don't go from zero to being an instant millionaire. It takes time – how long is up to you, but ultimately if you practice daily and consciously at any new belief or habit, for 21 days in a row, you can change your conditioning.

1 2 3 4 5 ... 11 12 13 14 15 16 17 18 19 20 21

REMEMBER

IT TAKES
AT LEAST

21 DAYS

TO FORM A
NEW HABIT!

1 2 3 4 5 6 7 8 9 10 11 12 13 14 15 16 17 18 19 20 21

The science of habit formation

For many people looking to form a habit, a common tactic is to ask what habitual learning is for successful people.

Mason Currey did just this in his book *Daily Rituals: How Artists Work.* He found that the secret to habit formation lies in knowing what works for YOU. This is what habitual learning is for successful people, so think back to what has worked for you in the past. There's no secret to habit formation in this respect; it's like happiness in that we're just all different!

How long does it take?

A common suggestion is 21 days. However, the amount of time it takes to form a new habit really just depends on what the habit is. Psychologist Jeremy Dean found that when he asked people to choose an everyday behaviour to turn into a new habit, it took on average 66 days. For those who decided to drink a glass of water after breakfast every day, this behaviour became automatic after 20 days. For those who decided to eat a piece of fruit with lunch, it took at least twice as long to turn that into a habit. One participant who vowed to do 50 sit-ups after morning coffee still hadn't formed this habit after 84 days.

Interestingly, it was found that earlier repetitions were most beneficial in forming the new habit, meaning the gains gradually lost momentum over time. So, whilst deciding to drink a glass of water every day might only take 21 days to become a habit, other behaviours can take much longer.

FOR THINGS TO
CHANGE YOU HAVE
TO CHANGE.
FOR THINGS TO
GET BETTER YOU
HAVE TO GET
BETTER!

~ Simon Stepsys ~

Quick Daily Habits For A Positive Mindset

01 Read personal development books daily for 30 minutes minimum

02 Delete, block and ban negativity from your life

03 Follow successful people

04 For every negative thought, replace with 11 positive thoughts

05 Commit with your mind, body and spirit

06 Focus on what you want

07 Embrace challenges as part of daily life

08 Remember you have a choice. Choose positivity

If you want to change your mindset fast, you have to do these things fast. You need to fill your life with everything to do with positivity, success, and successful people.

Study successful people and copy what they do.

Here are the key daily actions for a success mindset, which will lead you to a successful, happy and fulfilling life.

01 Read personal development books daily for 30 minutes minimum

Read self-development books written by successful people. Ideally, do 15 minutes to start your day off in a positive way and 15 minutes before bed at night.

That way you'll be planting positive thoughts into your mindset before you drift off to sleep. This is very powerful as your subconscious will soak up the new, positive ways of thinking and your brain will do the work for you whilst you're asleep.

If you have more time to dedicate to reading, then great – things will transform faster.

READERS ARE LEADERS!

My recommended top TEN reading list:

1. *The Master Key System* – by Charles F. Haanel

2. *Think and Grow Rich* – by Napoleon Hill

3. *The Science of Getting Rich* – by Wallace D Wattles

4. *The Power of Your Subconscious Mind* – by Dr Joseph Murphy

5. *Mindset. Money. Millionaire* – by Simon Stepsys

6. *Feel the Fear and Do It Anyway* – by Susan Jeffers

7. *How to Win Friends and Influence People* – by Dale Carnegie

8. *The Secret* – by Rhonda Byrne

9. *You Were Born to Win* – by Bob Proctor

10. *The 4-Hour Working Week* – by Tim Ferriss

The person you will be in five years is based on the books you read and the people you surround yourself with today

02 Delete, block and ban negativity from your life

If you're going to watch a film, watch something inspirational. Delete, block and ban negativity from your life.

This may seem harsh, but you may have to speak to people and let them know you don't want to be around negatives anymore. If you experience negative people on Facebook or other social media platforms, give them a warning and if they continue, delete, block and ban them.

You'll be amazed how your life starts to become positive. Turn off the news. Turn off the TV, and the radio too. Don't read the newspapers. They're mostly full of negativity. You're being brainwashed, even if you don't think you are. Even if the news is on in the background, your subconscious can hear every word – whether it's the TV, radio, or other people. If they haven't got smiling faces, get away. Practice this daily and you'll be amazed at how things turn around!

03 Follow successful people

...either on social media, or go to places where successful people go. It's really quite basic and easy, but it's also easy *not* to do. Like eating an apple every day, it's easy not to do it despite knowing it's good for you. Choose what is good for you.

04 For every negative thought, replace with 11 positive thoughts

You attract more of what you think about. If you think about positivity and success, you'll attract more of it. So it's crucial that you replace negative thoughts with at least 11 positive ones. This might seem extreme, and I used to replace every negative thought with at least 3 positive thoughts, but I was talking to a wiser man one day and he suggested upping that to 11. After I thought about it, it made a lot of sense. Apply this to your life and watch it transform; you'll be amazed at how it makes you feel – and feeling is everything.

This is really powerful. It's a habit; I've been studying personal development all my life. Terrible things have happened in my life, however I immediately see the positive – I would otherwise attract negative universal energy. It's incredible when you get this working in your favour. Just watch *The Secret* and you'll see what I mean.

05 Commit with your mind, body and spirit

There are 3 parts to us as humans: the body, the mind and the spirit. Work hard on each of these elements.

Work hard in a positive way – and maintain your dedication. Work on the mindset, the spiritual world, and the body. Look after each element and you'll create the conditions for a positive life.

The mind has the power to plug into the spiritual world. Plug into the universal world and its abundant energy. If you want something, keep it simple – just ask for it. And believe it will happen. You'll be amazed at what comes next. So if you want that Porsche, ask the universe for it and it will deliver. It might seem crazy as you're reading this right now but trust me, if you want it bad enough your mind will deliver it to you. It's the same

06 Focus on what you want

with anything you want. Just believe it and it's yours.
Most people don't even know what they want. So write down
what you want. Spend a good couple of hours on what you want
to achieve in life and when you want to achieve it by. Remember
you have one life: live it. You can have anything you want... Do
you want that Yacht in Monaco? It's yours. Do you want to be
around positive people in life? You can have this too. Do you
want to travel the world first class? You can do it! Just ask the
universe and it's yours.

It sounds great, doesn't it? Well, I can assure you, it is great! It's
phenomenal. All of this just from using the power of your mind.
Believe and trust in yourself; trust in the universe. And it is all
yours.

WANT IT?
WORK FOR IT!

This is what I want

There are no limits to the things you may want. Now you're going to be spending time exploring the things you feel you WANT, and WHY. For this exercise, I urge you to set aside some time where you can be alone, be quiet and really listen to your thoughts.

Things I feel I WANT right now:	WHY I want them:
1...	....
2...	....
3...	....
4...	....
5...	....
6...	....
7...	....
8...	....
9...	....
10...	....

Take a photo of this page, print it out and put it in a place where you will see it every day. Keep this list as a reminder of what you desire and what you want. DO NOT CONTINUE READING UNTIL YOU'VE COMPLETED THIS ACTIVITY.

IF YOU DON'T TAKE RISKS YOU DON'T DRINK CHAMPAGNE!

~ Simon Stepsys ~

07 Embrace challenges as part of daily life

Is your life going to be perfect? Of course not.

Things are going to happen in life that are beyond your control – you'll have challenges. Are you going to overcome them? Yes you are. Especially when you have the mindset skills. From every negative there will be a positive, and remember, where there is a positive there is always a negative. You can't have God without the Devil, and you can't have life without death. It's how you deal with them both that matters. Look for the positives and learn from the negatives. The universe will give you more of the positives if your mind is aligned to seek them out.

08 Remember you have a choice. Choose positivity

So remember...You can choose negative or positive. If you choose negative then you will attract more negativity to you and you won't feel so great as a result, but if you focus on positive you'll get positive energy out into the universe and you get more of that back. It's very important that you understand the importance of a positive mindset.

FEAR AND DOUBT. You MUST do what you fear and doubt! It's the only way to conquer them both!

Negativity will hold you back all your life. Over 85% of the things you worry about will never happen. Think about that, what a waste of time and energy that could be spent on other things.

Focus on what you want to happen, and what you want in life. Get the feeling of already owning what you want and it's only a matter of time before you will have it. How fast you get it is up to you.

Time dwelling on the things you want is time well spent. So don't feel you're wasting time thinking about the things you want because you're not: most people don't have the time to think because they're in the rat race – some people work 12-hour days. They come home shattered, have dinner, watch TV and collapse into bed. It's monotonous, mind-numbing and in my opinion quite depressing.

In the next section we'll look at discovering your 'Why' – the ultimate driver behind everything you do. Understanding your 'Why' is crucial. But first, let's discover your vision.

Your income will be an average of the 5 people you associate with...

Hang around 5 negative people and you'll become the 6th.

Hang around 5 millionaires and you'll become the 6th!

Vision Boards

Let's help you to get *really* clear about your vision.

To live in your vision multiple times daily...

I want you to create a Vision Board **RIGHT NOW!**

Here's what to do

Go into your local newsagents and buy a copy of all the magazines relating to your passion: this could be travel, homes, cars, bikes, personal development or yachts. Buy whatever gets you passionate!

Next, get yourself a MASSIVE piece of card. I suggest going to your local art shop for this and choosing the biggest size you can get your hands on. A1 or bigger if possible.

When you get home, look through the magazines and cut out all of the photos that impress your mind. Glue them to your Vision Board.

You can take this a step further, like I did. Print off some photos of yourself. Cut out your head from these photos and place yourself in that car, that home or whatever it is you've selected on your board. This lets you see yourself living in your vision, whatever it is: having money, freedom, being surrounded by successful people, having the things you want, driving the car of your dreams, or living in the house of your dreams.

Lastly, hang your Vision Board on a wall where you will see it every day. People who lack vision tend to return to their roots, so be sure to meditate on your Vision Board daily: in the morning, in the evening, and especially before you go to sleep.

I guarantee: this is so POWERFUL.

IF MY MIND CAN CONCEIVE IT, AND MY HEART CAN BELIEVE IT, THEN I CAN ACHIEVE IT

~ MUHAMMAD ALI ~

ALWAYS PRACTISE ON MANIFESTING THE FEELING OF ALREADY HAVING IT! LIVE IN YOUR VISION DAILY

~ SIMON STEPSYS ~

Chapter 3

DISCOVER YOUR WHY

WHAT DO YOU WANT?

DISCOVER YOUR WHY – WHAT DO YOU WANT?

CHAPTER
03

Why do so many people fail to achieve their goals? There's so much advice around that it's difficult to know which goal-setting practices really are the most useful.

So I'd like to share, through my own experimentation over the years regarding what helps to keep me focused, the goal-setting tips that are worth your time.

But first I'd like to tell you a story, taken from Darren Hardy's book *Living Your Best Year Ever...*

> *In the Andes Mountains, there were two warring tribes that not-so-peacefully co-existed – one that lived in the lowlands and the other high in the mountains. One day, the mountain people invaded the lowlanders, plundering and kidnapping a baby from the village. They vanished with the child and took her back up into the mountains.*
>
> *The lowlanders – pushed to action at the disappearance of one of their own – didn't*

know how to climb the mountain. They didn't know any of the trails that the mountain people used, and they didn't know where to find the mountain people or how to track them in the steep terrain.

Even so, they sent out their best party of fighting men to climb the mountain and bring the baby home.

The men first tried one method of climbing and then another. They tried one trail and then another. After several days of effort, however, they had climbed only a few hundred feet. Feeling hopeless and helpless, the lowlander men decided that the cause was lost, and they prepared to return to their village below. As they were packing their gear for the descent, they saw the baby's mother walking toward them. They realised that she was coming down the mountain that they hadn't figured out how to climb. They saw that she had the baby strapped to her back. How could that be?

One man greeted her and said, "We couldn't climb this mountain. How did you do this when we, the strongest and most able men in the village, couldn't do it?"

She looked intently at him and said, "It wasn't your baby."

WHEN YOU FIND YOUR 'WHY' YOU'LL FIND YOUR WAY

Your 'why'

The 90 Day Challenge will feel lonely without its why. So what *is* your 'why'?

Your 'why' is what feels authentically driven for YOU.

Many of us set goals that we know we want to achieve, but we don't sit down to really consider why that is. Why do we want a more successful business? Why do we want to quit our job? Why do we want to be more productive? Why do we want to lose weight?

The 'why' was the single most important driving factor in how the mother in the story got her baby back – and it's something we see in success stories day after day.

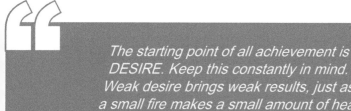

> The starting point of all achievement is DESIRE. Keep this constantly in mind. Weak desire brings weak results, just as a small fire makes a small amount of heat
>
> ~ Napoleon Hill ~

If you're finding yourself falling short of achieving the things you want in life, there's most likely a disconnection between saying you want something (whatever that is) and the steps you're taking to achieve it. That gap, that disconnection, is you not knowing your 'why'. This is where your motivation to actually go and get the things you want comes from.

If you don't already know what it is, here's how to find your 'why':

First, write down the things you want to achieve, and WHY they are important to you. This can be one sentence or a bullet-point list of reasons.

Things I want to achieve in life (my ambitions)	WHY I want them:
1..	....
2..	....
3..	....
4..	....
5..	....

Identify what you believe to be true 1

To be authentic, you need to live your own truth and not someone else's.

Is this the reason why you really want something? Or is it what someone else wants? Does it resonate with your core values?

What is your emotional connection to it?

The faith that you have will stabilise you through thick and thin – but your faith can only come out of the things you believe. If it's not your belief, your emotional connection, your 'why', you won't unconsciously have faith in it or be drawn to it.

The 'why' that is true to you will sustain you and keep you going when you hit bumps in the road – something you'll experience plenty of if you're following your dreams. Follow these 4 steps to really dig into your 'why'.

IF YOU
THINK BIG
THEN IT'S
GOING TO
BE BIG

~ Emeril Lagasse ~

Make sure it's big enough

2

WHY do you need a big enough 'why'?

You need a big enough 'why' in order to stick with anything. Why is it THE most important 'why' on your list of goals? The key here is self-determination, and it's something you can only find if your goals mean something to you.

Make sure the ways you can reach it are sustainable

3

I've written about creating new habits in the past; the key is that they must be sustainable. If your 'why' is really far away – a very long-term goal – it will most likely be too difficult to sustain and therefore attain. This is why breaking goals down is important.

It has to make you happy

4

Do you enjoy your 'why' in the moment? How do you feel when you're doing it – physically and mentally? Does it give you more physical energy and mental fuel? Pay attention to your body and you'll be surprised what you can learn about yourself.

SET HUGE GOALS:

What is your goal for TODAY?..

....

What are your goals for THIS WEEK?...

....

What are your goals for THIS MONTH?...

....

What are your goals for ONE YEAR?..

....

What are your goals for TWO YEARS?...

....

What are your goals for FIVE YEARS?..

....

What are your goals for TEN YEARS?...

....

Work backwards from your 'why'

Let's take a simple example. You want to lose weight because you want to be physically fitter and healthier. You think this will make you happier. Visualise this goal; really see the victory. What will you have to do to get there? Work backwards from your 'why'...

First, you'll need to start exercising to be physically fitter. So you could join a local gym, attend a set amount of classes per week which incorporate both cardio and strength training. You could pick classes that you'll enjoy and will be happy doing.

Second, you'll need to eat better to be physically healthier, so you can plan a meal you'll enjoy for every night of the week, buy the ingredients and cook it.

Third, you'll need to work around your existing weekly plans. You visualise yourself sat at the dinner table eating a healthy meal after work, but when did you work out? Would you be exercising afterwards? In the morning? It might work better

You must focus on abundance to bring more abundance to you
~ The Secret ~

> *ATTENTION!!*
> *WHILST YOU'RE WAITING,*
> *SOMEBODY ELSE IS DOING IT!!!*

for you to exercise before work, because you enjoy evenings relaxing. Working out every evening would make you unhappy – the opposite of your why. So, you set your goal accordingly by getting up an hour earlier in the morning, to exercise and shower.

Goal-setting backwards like this helps you to really visualise your goals. You're thinking about the why – to be physically fitter and healthier and therefore happier – rather than the surface goal which is just to lose weight. Picturing yourself happy is why you're thinking about the types of exercise you'll have to do and the meals you'll need to plan. You're not deciding to just cut down on unhealthy food and do classes you're not motivated to go to, because you won't enjoy that.

It's all about bringing it back to what makes you happy.

Break goals down into actionable steps

This goes hand-in-hand with my last point. When you're working backwards with big goals, break them down into actionable

COMPLAINING HAS NO VALUE

IF YOU'RE COMPLAINING ABOUT NOT
HAVING ENOUGH MONEY...WORK MORE

WORK MORE WORK MORE

WANT GOLD? WORK
WANT BLING? WORK
WANT A FERRARI? WORK
WANT A ROLLS ROYCE? WORK
WANT JETS OR A YACHT? WORK
WANT FREEDOM? WORK

WORK WORK WORK

WORK LIKE YOU'RE POOR

~ Simon Stepsys ~

steps. You'll notice that I did that with my example.

"When it is obvious that the goals cannot be reached, don't adjust the goals, adjust the action steps" – **Confucius**

However, this book is about BUSINESS, so let's get back on track. Just remember that successful goals are SMART: Specific, Measurable, Attainable, Realistic and Timely.

Bring your 'why' back when times get tough

"He who has a why can endure any how" – **Frederich Nietzsche**

When you're breaking a goal down into individual tasks and activities, you'll easily lose focus or get distracted. All the little things you need to do to get there will discourage you and you might want to give up. This is where you can use your 'why' as a tool to keep yourself motivated and on track. Keep your eye on the prize!

Do something today that your future self will thank you for
~ Unknown ~

> *Money is not the most important thing in the world. Love is. Fortunately, I love money*
>
> ~ Jackie Mason ~

Every time you find yourself losing focus, ask yourself 'why'.

As the story previously showed, the person who has a vivid, compelling and white-hot burning reason *why* will always defeat the best of the best at doing the *how*.

Find supportive people

Your 'why' resonates with your core values. Who else shares these values? Those who do will support you, and you'll want people like that to remind you of your 'why' when you're struggling. Building a team will also help you to stay accountable.

Round-up

"People with goals succeed because they know where they are going, it's as simple as that" **– Earl Nightingale**

Taking a moment to discover – or re-discover – your 'why' can work wonders. For your motivation, your self-esteem, your confidence and the likelihood of achieving success.

Find your 'why' by listening to your own truth, by making your 'why' big enough, sustainable enough and enjoyable enough to be worthy of your time.

Then set some goals you can really reach using your 'why'. Work backwards, break everything down to make success a reality, use it as fuel and find supportive people.

Read your why's at least daily – preferably just before setting a to-do list and first thing in the morning.

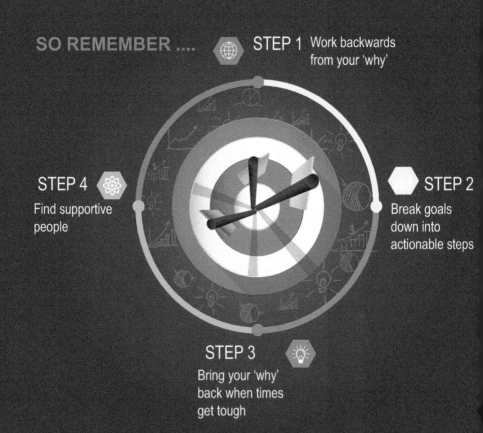

SO REMEMBER ....

STEP 1 Work backwards from your 'why'

STEP 2 Break goals down into actionable steps

STEP 3 Bring your 'why' back when times get tough

STEP 4 Find supportive people

Chapter 4

PREPARING FOR THE 90 DAY CHALLENGE

The right attitude very rarely leads to the wrong action

~ Tom Ziglar ~

PREPARING FOR THE 90 DAY CHALLENGE

CHAPTER
04

This chapter explains in detail exactly what you need to do in order to put The 90 Day Challenge into action. However, before we get to that there are some basic steps that you'll need to take in order to get prepared.

If you don't follow these steps now, you may find that implementing your daily actions takes longer than you anticipated. I want to do everything I can to ensure that when you come to implement The 90 Day Challenge, the process is as smooth and easy as possible. This way, you're even more likely to continue and succeed for the 90 days – and beyond.

Let me re-emphasise: you'll be reaching out in at least 3 to 5 ways daily

So, what does the preparation include?

Well, one of the suggestions in the next chapter is that you create a video daily and post it onto social media. This is great, but if you don't already have your social media accounts set up with a decent amount of followers, when it comes to taking that specific action you're going to have more work to do.

Let me be clear: this is not rocket science. We're aiming for simplicity, so do yourself a favour and get organised in advance.

This preparatory chapter lays the foundations for your 90 days, but it doesn't mean you can't get started sooner. For example, whilst you're setting up your social media accounts you can get started with other aspects of the plan, such as sending out a mailing to your prospect list. You can pick up the phone and speak to your prospects, or you can put an advert in the local paper.

Do not let 'excuse-iutus' get in the way. Watch what your mind is telling you about why you 'can't' do something. For example, 'I can't produce a video today because I don't have a YouTube

> *What you think, you become. What you feel, you attract. What you imagine, you create*
>
> ~ Buddha ~

> *Where focus goes, energy flows*
> ~ Tony Robbins ~

account' is actually: 'I won't produce a video'. And is that really true, that you 'won't'? Why won't you? Is it because you don't want to, or are you masking fear by saying you can't? The likelihood is that you are masking fear. And my advice to you is to challenge that fear – are you really going to let some nerves get in the way of you and your goal of doubling your business? I didn't think so.

It takes five minutes to set up a YouTube account, and only five more minutes to record a video and upload it. In just ten minutes you can have a video out there! The day after, you can record a new 30-second video, upload to YouTube and Facebook, and that's two of your actions for the day taken care of! BOOM!

Let's get started with the preparation

On the following pages you'll find a list of important tools that I and a lot of my students have used. I highly recommend them – especially if you're serious about making big money (by which I mean at least 6/7 figures a year).

1 | Set up a Capture/Squeeze Page

This is a specific type of landing page which allows you to collect the email addresses of your prospects in response to an advert or promotion. Your Capture page needs to be easy to complete; many Internet marketers now only ask for email address on their Capture pages. Ask for less information and you'll tend to get more subscribers. You want to be sending enough traffic to your Capture page to get 20–40 opt-ins per day. If you're doing this, you should be getting 1–2 people joining your business daily!

2 | Automate Your Business

This is the 21st century! Link your Capture page to an autoresponder, and build your list daily! You don't need huge lists to build massive teams. From 20 to 40 new daily subscribers, you should easily be able to convert at least 1 to 2 new team members. In your follow-up emails, make an IRRESISTABLE offer with a deadline to get your subscribers to take action on that day. Something like, "FREE special Bonus worth more than $500 for the next two people who join my team today by midnight!" You can also offer a free gift, course, eBook, audio, a free report, tips, access to an interview or even free coaching with you. A one-to-one coaching call would be a great one to offer. The value you put on this is up to you: $50, $500 or even more.

Drive traffic by advertising your Capture page EVERYWHERE!

" 95 % of people in life never get
what they want. Why? Most
people don't even know
what they want!
You NEED to know what you
want! "

3 | Get Blogging

If you look at all the top marketers in direct sales, almost all of them have their own dedicated blog, including me! Why? It's all about branding you! Through your blog, people will get to KNOW, LIKE and TRUST you. I blog regularly: often up to 3 times a day. If you have no idea how to set up your own blog, then no worries at all: you can outsource this. Go to sites like peopleperhour.com, fiverr.com, upwork.com, elance.com and guru.com.

4 | Use The Big 7 Social Media Platforms

Get a profile on each of the Big 7 social media platforms listed on the following page. Remember this is business not a hobby; be careful what you're posting and how you're writing. Of course, let your personality shine through but be professional about it. Think about how you want to be perceived and what you want your customers to see. And crucially, choose an appropriate picture as your profile image.

5 | Get Some Business Cards & Dropcards

These are your advertisement, and in the next section I'm going to be sharing with you how you can use them to your advantage. Ensure that you have a good stash of these ready in advance of The 90 Day Challenge!

THE BIG 7
SOCIAL MEDIA PLATFORMS

OPEN ACCOUNTS WITH ALL OF THESE SOCIAL MEDIA PLATFORMS

1 Facebook
More than one billion people are active on Facebook

2 YouTube
One third of the world is on Youtube

3 Twitter
83% of the World's Leaders are on Twitter

4 Linkedin
There are 2 new LinkedIn members per second

5 Instagram
Instagram users generate 3.5 billion likes per day

Pinterest
88% of people have purchased a product they have pinned....
and is my person favorite as a 7+

THINK
KEEP IT PROFESSIONAL.
IT'S BUSINESS NOT PLEASURE

6 Snapchat
It's been beaten only by Facebook. Snapchat has become so popular now Facebook is the only rival which can be

7 Skype
Skype has 360 million users worldwide & 30% of Skype users use Skype for business purposes

ACT NOW
SET UP ACCOUNTS TO THESE MEDIA PLATFORMS

6 | Headlines

Know how to write a good headline for your adverts and blogs. Newspapers know the importance of a great headline, and you need to know this too. Whether you're writing a blog post or putting an advert in a paper, you need to spend time ensuring that your headline is right. 'How to' headlines work brilliantly. For example, 'How to make money on the Internet', or 'How to lose weight fast'. These are just two examples, but you'll be starting to get the idea. Headlines that give important information that can solve people's challenges are going to get attention.

Did you know?

Over 90% of all of the responses to the ads you write will come from the headline. If you have a poor headline, no one reads any further. I advise you to look at newspapers and get ideas.

Write ATTENTION-GRABBING headlines.

Over 90% of your success in advertising comes down to your headline! Write this down on a Post-It note and stick it on your forehead. It's that important!

Practice writing powerful headlines DAILY.

AIDA FORMULA

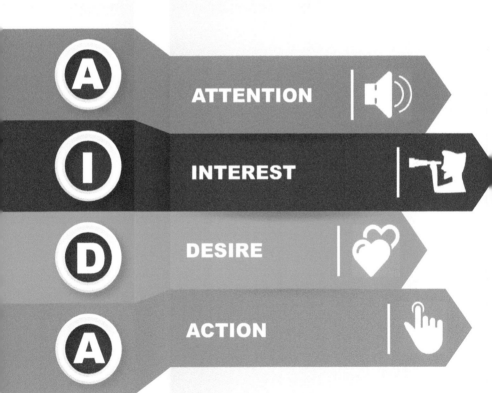

A ATTENTION

I INTEREST

D DESIRE

A ACTION

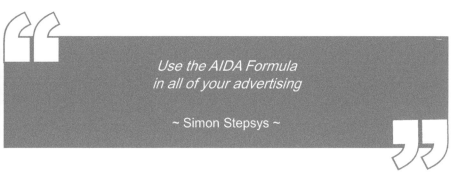

Use the AIDA Formula
in all of your advertising

~ Simon Stepsys ~

Use the AIDA formula to generate great content:

A = Attention. Write strong, compelling headlines, such as 'How to...'

I = Interest. Provide an interesting sub-heading to encourage the reader to continue.

D = Desire. Create the desire for more information... For example, in an advert where you're looking for entrepreneurs to join a business opportunity, 'Earnings potential truly unlimited' is going to generate a LOT of interest.

A = Action. For example, 'to learn more click here or call'.

Every time you write an advert, consider these elements.

Blogging

The importance of posting blog content regularly should not be underestimated, but I understand that it may seem daunting at first. Most people in business do not expect to have to also be a great writer, and this is why I've dedicated a significant part of this chapter to the process of blog writing.

It doesn't have to be daunting – in fact it can be quite enjoyable once you know the basic rules. I teach that everyone in business should be generating content each and every day. Knowing how to generate good-quality content for your blog posts is actually easier than you think.

Those who write content regularly will know and understand that once you get going, the ideas flow freely. I write up to three blog posts daily, but by the evening I've often written down another six ideas for blog posts to the following day.

In order to get started with writing content for blog posts, you'll need somewhere to begin. Here is a quick-start guide to generating ideas.

It's never been about the money, it's about the options it provides

~ Unknown ~

Look back at what has worked in the past

If you've written blog posts before, you might want to analyse the statistics and see which topics and posts have been the most popular. This will give you hints and clues as to what your audience wants to read about. Once you have this information, you can explore new ways to present it, by giving it a new angle or a twist.

Take a look at comments on your blogs

Perhaps some of your blog posts have comments... these can be invaluable pieces of information as the questions asked can lead you to content opportunities. If you have no raw material of your own to go at, look at blog posts by people who are similar to you and what you offer and see what questions they're addressing.

Look at social media forums for inspiration

Take a look at comment threads on social media posts that are relevant to you and your customer base, and then write blog posts that answer some of the comment queries or concerns.

What questions are people asking? What are the most common headaches, trends and themes you can pick out? And crucially, what is it that you can offer by way of help or service to people in response?

> *INSANITY IS DOING THE SAME THING OVER AND OVER AGAIN AND EXPECTING A DIFFERENT RESULT!*

Go back to basics

Back in the days before the Internet, before Google was the place to go in order to learn and do research, people used to sit around tables and brainstorm ideas. There's nothing like getting together with a group of like-minded people – particularly those who are on your wavelength and who are open-minded to new ideas. Spend an hour generating ideas; you'll be amazed at what you come up with.

Blogging as the new marketing channel

You need to get into the mindset of seeing your blog as one of the fundamental ways that you promote your business.

This is because business blogging is essentially a marketing channel. It is a (relatively) new way to raise awareness of who you are and what you do – rather like the older forms of advertising such as TV commercials or newspaper advertorials.

Blogging about your business gives you the opportunity to write about what you do in a relatively quick and easy way, and its aim is to generate discussions that turn into leads, which ultimately convert into business.

Blogging for growth

So your blog is there to support and promote business growth by driving more quality traffic to your website.

It is not the primary function of your business – that is your product or service.

This means the content must be professional, accurate, well written and easy to understand. Every time you produce content for your blog and upload it, it is one more opportunity for search engines to find you and one more opportunity for people to engage with you and share your content on social media.

Writing content about topics of interest is definitely worth doing, firstly because it gives you a great opportunity to practice your writing. The brain is like any other muscle in your body; the

IF YOU KEEP DOING WHAT YOU'RE DOING., YOU'LL KEEP GETTING WHAT YOU'RE GETTING!

~ Simon Stepsys ~

more you use it for a specific purpose, the better and stronger it becomes.

So, why not practise your skills on a personal blog, so that when you come to write content for your business one, you feel more confident and competent?

Top tips for writing an amazing blog post

Structuring and writing a blog post – like all other types of writing – is a skill.

And whilst truly great writing talent can't be taught, writing that is 'good enough' definitely can. I've learned the techniques involved in writing in an appealing style, and now I'd like to share them with you.

I'm going to be sharing some top tips for creating content that speaks to your readers, paints a picture, tells a story and inspires action!

> *At the end of the next 25 years you can have 25 years' experience or you can have one year's experience 25 times. It's a matter of choice.*
>
> *~ Simon Stepsys ~*

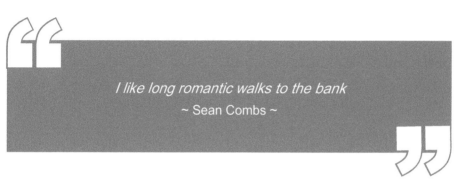

I like long romantic walks to the bank
~ Sean Combs ~

Captivate

Do not underestimate the importance of your introduction. Did you know that 38% of people who click on your blog post will leave after reading only the first few words? This means that you have seconds – no, make that nanoseconds – to capture your reader and get them to stay on your page. So make your opening paragraph one that will captivate, inspire or excite them enough that they literally HAVE to keep reading.

Make a promise and stick to it

Empathise with your readers' hopes and dreams, as well as their struggles. Or, talk about a common problem and why it's important to fix it. Then make a promise to solve that problem if they continue reading to the end.

Build a relationship

By this, I ultimately mean know your audience and then write to them as real human beings. Your blog is not a diary – its purpose isn't an outpouring of emotions – but it is an opportunity for you to share your knowledge, wisdom and offering to your potential customers. Find a writing voice and style that you're comfortable and relaxed using, and the content will flow more naturally and sound more authentic too.

Use case studies and examples

Nothing brings a piece of writing to life better than a real-life case study or personal example. To illustrate this, can you remember how many direct referrals I have personally sponsored in the last two and a half years? And did this inspire you to want to read on and find out how I achieved this? My guess is that you answered 'over 5000' and 'YES'!

Understand that everyone is busy

Remember how I told you that you'll lose many of your readers after the first few words? Well you'll be much less likely to do so if you appreciate that they are busy people who don't have hours to spare to wade through long, dense paragraphs of technical

Believe you can and you're halfway there

~ Theodore Roosevelt ~

information that's difficult to follow. Avoid jargon, keep paragraphs short, use bullet points and headings to break up text and make sure that you always bring your reader back to the key points.

Some guidance on Search Engine Optimisation (SEO)

Driving traffic to your website through appropriate Search Engine Optimisation (SEO) is not an art; it's a science. And if you follow these simple strategies, you are more likely to see greater results from your blogging efforts.

You need to get smart about a few factors:

Choose your keyword wisely and make it work for you

Make sure that your keyword appears within your heading, then the first line of your article and the last line too. You'll also need to ensure that your keyword appears throughout the blog or web posting regularly. For the best search engine optimisation (SEO) results, you also need to ensure that your blog or article has a keyword density of about 3–5%.

Use bold and italics on your keyword

This technique is another you can use to boost your rankings and drive traffic to your website.

Use your keyword in your image uploads

On a Wordpress blog, you will have the option of adding an image and a caption. Get your keyword into the caption as well as the title of the image. In addition, you can use the 'Alt Text' function to place your keyword in one more time.

Link to other articles in your blog

It's no longer enough to have links to external articles on your blog; you also need to be linking back to your own blog as well. It's important here that the post you link back to is relevant, otherwise you can confuse and alienate your reader. After all, your primary aim is to get traffic to your website – you don't have to move away from providing good-quality content that interests and educates your reader.

Chapter 5

100+ ACTIONS FOR YOU TO CHOOSE FROM

100+

**Here's the problem.
Most people are thinking about
what they don't want, and they're
wondering why it shows up over
and over again**

~ Rhonda Byrne ~

Spend 80% of your time on IPA (Income Producing Activities), and the other 20% on learning

In the pages that follow, I'm going to share with you over 100 Income Producing Activities (IPAs) in the form of marketing tips that are easy to understand and even easier to implement. These tips will become your reference guide for the whole of The 90 Day Challenge. So be sure to bookmark this page, making it as easy as possible to locate these tips. Carry this book around with you. Have it to hand. You're going to be returning to it for the next 90 days and beyond.

Managing your time

When you're growing your business, 80% of your time should be spent on IPAs. The other 20% is time set aside for your learning.

Say you have 100 minutes. Spend 20 minutes learning how to do something (for example blogging) and then 80 minutes actively doing that thing. Whatever that might be: making calls to prospects, placing adverts or getting content out there on the Internet.

I urge you to apply this principle as you begin The 90 Day Challenge.

Most people waste their time doing nothing. Don't be one of those people.

Spend 80% of your time on IPA, and the other 20% on learning

PASSIVE Marketing versus ACTIVE Marketing

Before I share the tips with you, it is VERY important that you understand the distinction between Passive and Active Marketing.

Some of the followinf tips are Active and some Passive. You need to aim for a balance between the two, but more importantly, you absolutely MUST ensure that you include Active forms of promoting your business.

Here's why...

Passive Marketing is where you put content out and then wait for a response. This could be a Facebook post, or a video or an advert. This activity is passive because once you've put the content out there, you have to wait for people to take action and contact YOU.

So what is Active Marketing?

This is where you are actively pursuing prospects – either by calling or messaging them directly. 'Headhunting' if you like.

This is a much faster way to build business.

I can guarantee that nearly all of you reading this book will want to take the Passive route, and this is the problem.

A willingness to pick up the phone and be Active is the differentiating factor between those who make it and those who don't. Do you want to pick up the phone? My guess is that about 5% of you do and the rest don't. Just be aware that those who do will have a much greater chance of making it big, because they either have no fear, or they're feeling the fear and doing it anyway!

Remember this: it shouldn't be a problem to pick up the phone if you have a good product or service to offer. Focus on the value.

I was trained to always focus on what's in it for the prospect, rather than what's in it for me. So as you prepare to pick up the phone, forget what you might receive in terms of money as a result of the call, and shift your energy, focus and attention onto helping the other person. That way, the message is, 'I have a solution that can help you to pay your debts off', or 'I can help you to free time in your day so that you can enjoy a better quality of life'. Then ask if they're interested and open to finding out more.

It's also good to bear in mind that by actively speaking with prospects, you're engaging in a sorting or sifting process. You're asking people if they're interested and open-minded enough to hear what you have to offer. What's great is that you'll get a clear response, and then you'll know whether to follow up with them at a later date or focus your energies elsewhere.

Let's work through an example of an ACTIVE day

You pick up the phone and you speak to three new prospects.

One of them is interested and two aren't.

Fantastic: you have one new interested person!

Now an example of a passive day

Let's say you do five actions.

You post videos on YouTube and Facebook, write and share a blog post, you put an ad on Craigslist and you send a Tweet out.

After doing all of these things, you could get zero response.

In fact, it would be very unusual if you got a response on the same day. Now compare it with the phone calls in the first example.

Who is building their business faster?

This is why I highly recommend that you do AT LEAST one ACTIVE Marketing task per day.

Call, actively pursue, or headhunt at least one new person each day.

Covering all bases

Of your 3–5 tasks per day I would encourage you to make at least one of these an Active task. You're probably starting to realise that there aren't actually that many Active methods – aside from directly calling and messaging people – whereas there are a lot of Passive methods.

Most people are taking the Passive route and so by doing something different, you're likely to stand out. I've been actively pursued many times by people who are brave enough to pick up the phone.

If you're doing your 3–5 tasks, and you pursue one person each day, your business will grow MUCH quicker.

So let's get really clear…

Posting 5 times on Facebook is Passive, and it is only ONE of your actions – not 5. You've still got 4 more to do. That's very important. Remember: Facebook posts, blogs and even paid adverts are all Passive actions.

With Active prospecting, starting with your own list of contacts, you get IMMEDIATE results. While the Passive approach could take many months or even years.

So, hold meetings, pursue people on the Internet (find them on social media) and contact them directly; actively use Skype or Facebook Messenger. Text your contacts by all means. But it still isn't as good as the phone call. You can also attend networking events and other business opportunities, and start speaking to people. Buy leads and call them. This is by far the best way to build your business; on a scale of one to ten, the phone call is ten out of ten!

Now, take a minute and ask yourself, which type of activity are you more comfortable with?

You're in your comfort zone with Passive activity. I'm here to challenge you to step outside of that. Do something different and watch results happen, FAST!

Five Active Marketing tasks are going to far out-perform five Passive ones. You could send an email to your list, post onto Facebook and place multiple ads daily, but this is the Passive approach. You may never hear anything from these activities.

If you actively pursue five people, you might get three who say 'No', one who says 'Maybe' and one 'Yes'. But that's still one 'Yes'!

Who is building faster? Active Marketing is instant. Those that take the Active route will build bigger and faster.

If you want it badly enough, you'll do it.

When you're actively recruiting and out there prospecting, you're connecting with people on a daily basis and following up. This is where you see immediate and fast results and how you will recruit people daily into your business.

In summary

As you go through The 90 Day Challenge, make sure at least one of your 3–5 is an Active task. If you speak to five new people in one day, then this would be a maximum score for that day.

Now imagine you did this for 90 days consecutively – that would be 450 people you've reached out to and spoken with. It would be impossible NOT to double your business in 90 days with that kind of activity. It's the truth. This is the absolutely truth. If you want to double your business, start actively pursuing. Start with your phone contacts and Facebook friends.

Most people will have at the very least 150 friends, but I want you to get into the Facebook groups and build up to 5000 friends – then you can actively pursue and reach out to ALL of them. There are loads of social networking sites that have huge numbers of members – I can guarantee you'll never be short of people to connect with.

Hold this in mind as you turn the page and read through the list of tips. Good luck – and most importantly, ENJOY!

Affirmation of the day:

"I AM A
MONEY
MAGNET"

The importance of POWERFUL Positive Affirmations...

"I am"… and the words that you say after them become a self-fulfilling prophecy. Say out loud:

I am successful, I am happy, I help and inspire others, I am healthy.

In other words, THINK positively!

Now look at the alternatives:

I am stupid, I am an idiot, I don't know anything, I'm useless.

Every time you have a conversation with yourself you have a choice: you can follow the negatives or switch to positives.

But remember: you will never be successful with a negative mindset.

I urge you to write down your affirmations:

I am successful, I am happy, I am healthy, I am positive, I inspire others, I provide great leadership. I make over 10K+ a month (or whatever amount you want).

The key is to find yourself a positive affirmation that you're comfortable with and that drives you. Write it down 20, 40, even

100 times daily. Get a nice pen and pad, enjoy the experience. I bought myself a nice moleskin notebook and pen to write down positive affirmations, goals, action plans. I then meditate and see myself achieving these.

I want you to imagine yourself flying first class, driving that Porsche, or speaking on stage and sharing your story of massive success. See yourself signing autographs for others, being photographed with people who aspire to live the life that you've built for yourself. Live in that feeling; see yourself in your dream home, on a beautiful beach; feel the sun on your back, looking good and feeling great.

Live in that vision

If you see it in your mind, you're going to hold it in your hand

~ Rhonda Byrne ~

Affirmations exercise

I want you to spend some time writing out positive affirmations below… Do not skip this exercise; it's LIFE-CHANGING!

I am ....

I am ....

I am ....

I am ....

I am ....

I am ....

I am ....

I am ....

I am ....

I am ....

I am ....

I am ....

I am ....

I am ....

I am ....

I am ....

I am ....

I am ....

I am ....

I am ....

YOU WILL ALWAYS GET WHAT YOU BELIEVE

GET ACTIVE!

Of your 3–5 Daily Action Tasks, I highly recommend
one of them be an Active task.

This means actively picking up the phone and actively
sending messages to prospects. This is Direct Sales, guys!

ACTIVELY pursue people.

Most people tend to use only Passive techniques,
and this is why they tend to get few results.
Attraction marketing takes time.

This is the truth.

Remember: if you want something badly enough, you will do it.

As an example: my personal top 5 recommendations for your 3–5 Daily Actions

1) Pick up the phone – take the ACTIVE marketing route and talk to a new person

2) Record and POST a video on YouTube then SHARE that video on Facebook, Twitter, LinkedIn, your blog and Tumblr!

3) Place an ad on one of the classified ad sites, such as Craigslist, Backpage or your local newspaper

4) Create a well-written Blog post. At least 400–500 words minimum in length. Once written, promote in AT LEAST 5 Facebook targeted groups, Tweet it, post it on LinkedIn, and Tumblr it! BE RELENTLESS!!!

5) Email your list daily with an update – include an IRRESISTIBLE special offer with a deadline

As you work through these actions, you may become aware of some resistance to spending money on your adverts. Remind yourself of this powerful affirmation: 'Every pound, euro or dollar I spend comes back to me TENFOLD!' I recommend that you build up a budget where you can be spending $10,000 dollars a month on marketing and promoting your business.

1) Pick up the phone. This method is by far the best to build your business, even if it is one of the oldest techniques. Pick up the phone and call your contacts. Think about it: if you have 90 contacts in your phone list (most people have many more) and you call one of these each day for 90 days, then that's 90 new people who will know about your business. Most of you reading this book will want to avoid the direct calling method, but it's a 10/10 activity and it is NUMBER ONE on my list for a reason. I strongly recommend that this action should make up one of your 3–5 each day. Do this and you'll get a BIG tick in your Action Tracker for that day.

When calling your prospects, just ask them, 'Are you open to looking at an exciting new business opportunity?' Or, 'Do you know of anyone who would be interested in making some serious extra money?' Keep it simple! IT IS!

2) Advertise on bank notes. Get a bank note and write a catchy headline on it, together with your website address. For example,

'Entrepreneurs Wanted, YourWebsite.com' (Capture page). You could even go a step further and get a specifically designed stamp made up and then stamp your message rather than write it. This is such a powerful activity when you think about how many people will see this note. Currency passes through the hands of many people each and every day, and so you never know who is going to get passed your note! Isn't that just phenomenal?

3) Facebook video. This doesn't have to be lengthy – just a quick video update about you and your business. Post it onto your Facebook page and in your groups. Ask people to Like, Comment and Share. In addition, you may want to do a Facebook Live video – that will really get you noticed and your audience talking!

4) Blog. I've gone into detail in Chapter 4 of this book about the importance of blogging and the ways in which you can optimise

your content for search engines. Blogs are so powerful; they allow your personality to shine through and let you connect directly with your reader. A good blog is 400–500 words minimum, and includes good-quality, well-written and researched content that is relevant and interesting to your readers. Always encourage them to comment and share your post at the end of each blog, and make sure you finish off with a link to your Capture page.

5) Promote your blog. Actively promote your blog post in at least 5 targeted Facebook groups daily. Put a tick in the box for today. Well done.

6) Join LinkedIn groups. Join targeted groups on LinkedIn and post adverts in those groups daily.

7) Leave drop cards. Leave at least 30 of your business or drop cards in bars, restaurants, cafes, on trains… anywhere that people may pick them up. Be sure that your cards display your advert and Capture page. Some examples of what you may want

FREE
100+
MARKETING
TIPS

to say include: Work From Home! Be Your Own Boss! Work Your Own Hours! Unlimited Earnings Potential!

8) Tweet your blog. **Tweet your blog posts daily. BOOM!**

9) Instagram. **Upload photographs to Instagram with up to ten hashtags that are relevant to your niche.**

10) YouTube videos. **Record a short video and post it onto your YouTube channel. Imagine if you did this for 90 days – this equals 90 videos about your business out there in the world! What's even more powerful is that if ten members of your team are doing this, that's 900 videos. WOW! You'll be flooding the Internet with your message. But how many people are actually doing it? Be sure of one thing: that you're doing it!! YOU ROCK!**

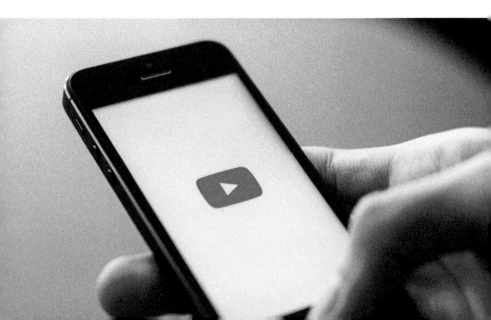

11) Comment on blogs. Find a blog that relates to your area of business and then leave a well-written, thoughtful comment of about 10–100 words in length. One is great, 3–5 is POWERFUL and gives you more exposure. Be positive and upbeat in your comments; don't criticise the author of the blog post or other people… People read the comments on blog posts and so this is a great method of getting you name out there… the key of course is to include a link to your Capture page or website so that people can make contact with you.

12) Comment on YouTube videos. YouTube is MASSIVE! I watch supercar videos and leave comments, simply congratulating the originator on a fantastic video, and then speaking directly to the other viewers with something along the lines of: 'If you haven't got the means to buy a car like this then follow this link' – and simply leave a link to your Capture page.

13) Freebies. Give people an incentive to make contact with you. Post out onto Facebook: 'Private message with your best email address and you'll receive a free guide to the 5 Best Ways to Make Money on the Internet'. (Of course, you'll need to offer something that you've written and is in your area of specialism.) Once they've made contact, send them a link to your Capture page and ask them to sign up. Everyone loves a freebie!

14) Easy-Hits-4U.com. Place an ad here. This site has over

1 million members, has delivered billions of ad views, and it has been established since 2003. Place ads daily! BOOM!

15) Text marketing. Text all of your contacts in your contact list with an exciting opportunity or offer: 'Finally! Anyone can work from home and create a massive income! For more details visit…' and then simply add a link to your Capture page. Give them a deadline for any offer you're promoting to encourage a quick response. You might want to consider using a specific app that will enable you to bulk text your contacts – Group TextPro is what I personally use. BulkSMS.com is also great. This is so basic but so effective. An easy tick!

16) Email your list daily. This is so easy to do; it takes two minutes and allows you to communicate with anyone who has expressed an interest in hearing from you. Send an email with a Special Offer and set a deadline for that Special Offer. Or send them a link to a new blog post that you've written.

17) Advertise on the back window of your car. There are many places you can put an ad on your car, the easiest being the back window. You'll need to use a strong headline and then simply state your Capture page address. For example, 'Work From

Home', 'Be Your Own Boss', and then 'visit www.YourWebsite. com' (your Capture page). You can go one step further and have your own number plate created, with your headline and your website Capture page on there too!

18) eBay advertising. Set up an account and place an advert on eBay. Think about it: eBay is absolutely full of buyers – buying is the main purpose of the site and so you'll be getting your message out to people who are already poised, credit card in hand, to part with some money! Put a tick in your box!

19) Advertise in shop windows. Build good relationships with your local retailers and place postcard-sized ads in shop windows. Many newsagents, hairdressers and takeaways have sections in their windows where people can place adverts, so take advantage! You never know, you might also be able to sign up the shop owner whilst you're there! One advert equals one of your daily actions.

20) Notice boards. Many other retailers will have a notice board where people can place adverts. Go and explore your local supermarket, GP surgery, coffee shop, or any other location in your town that may be willing to allow you to place an advert.

21) Roadside ads. You can put an advert at the side of the road with your headline and your website/Capture page. Something

like this would be perfect: 'Escape the Rat Race! www. yourwebsite.com'. Place your ad where traffic queues are likely. People will look around, see your ad, and... BOOM!

22) About.me. **Set up an About.me page – this helps you to brand yourself. I highly recommend that you put a link to your blog and Capture page on there, and then email your list to let them know about it!**

23) WhatsApp. **Build up your WhatsApp contact list and actively message at least one new person per day. You're doing great!**

24) Skype marketing. **Build your Skype list. If you haven't already, set yourself up with a Skype account and then join relevant groups. Instant Message the members of these groups daily. You've got to actively pursue people in order to be doing the business correctly. Direct message people and ask, 'Do you keep your options open?' To learn more about this, search on Google for Skype Marketing or watch some YouTube videos.**

25) Fiverr.com. **Place a daily advert on Fiverr.com and be sure to target your niche. You can do this multiple times! One advert equals one of your daily actions.**

26) Target your niche. Via whatever means – LinkedIn, Facebook, or other social media platform, actively seek out people who work within your niche. Contact them and ask them, 'Do you keep your options open?' If you don't ask, you don't get. It's all a numbers game. The more 'No's' you get, the closer you are to a 'Yes!'

27) BuySellAds.com. A fantastic and powerful site to place your advertising banners. Absolutely brilliant. Place one new ad on here per day and put a tick on your Daily Action Tracker.

28) ClixSense.com. A great place to advertise your business. Place new ads on this site daily and put a tick on your Action Tracker.

29) NeoBux.com. Another fantastic site to advertise your website; place a new ad on here daily. Well done – you're on you're way to DOUBLING your business!

30) WarriorForum.com. Direct message other marketers in the groups. You can also leave comments on posts – just be sure to leave a link back to your website or Capture page.

31) BigAdvertising.co.uk. A place to buy leads (mention Simon Stepsys for a big discount). Make contact by phone or text, and follow up. Always remember: the fortune is in the follow-up.

32) SoloAdsGuru.com. **THE best place to buy Solo Ads and one of the fastest and easiest ways to get traffic to your website. Open an account and then connect with one of the advertisers and book a Solo Ad. Do it now! Do this daily and build your list on steroids!**

33) Advertise on your car number plate. **You can simply use a headline and link to your Capture page. Drive around a busy area to clock up one of your 3–5 daily actions.**

34) Snapchat. **Open a Snapchat account and start to build up your contact list. Put your Snapchat username in the footer of all your emails, blog posts and on your Facebook page. Direct message people daily. You're doing great!**

35) Coffee meetings. **Create an event as a coffee meeting. Decide on the date and location, open an event on Facebook and then invite all of your friends. Even if just a few people turn up, you are actively prospecting those people, and it's a nice, informal way to build relationships. Gold star activity.**

36) Craigslist.com. **An online platform that offers the opportunity to place classified ads as well as being an online forum.**

Someone wishing to use this website to their advantage may post a simple advert on a daily basis asking people to "get in touch" if they "want financial freedom". With regards to the forums, people can also leave comments on these, with a link to their website or Capture page. Users have the option of posting anonymously.

37) Backpage.com. A classified advertising site. You can use this in the same way as Craigslist; by posting adverts on a daily basis. Again this can be simple, just asking people to get in touch if they desire financial freedom.

38) Gumtree.com. A great classified ads site. With nearly 8 million visitors per month, this is a great place to put up your advert. There is also the option to promote your ads – giving you better visibility. One ad equals one of your actions.

39) Oodle.com. Unlike Craigslist, this doesn't require users to post content personally and manually. It also incorporates social networks into its classifieds, whereas Craigslist is more anonymous.

40) ClassifiedAds.com. Another free classified ads website with the option of renewing ads, uploading pictures and adding links. You can also select your own expiration deadline – from one week to nine months. No sign-up required equals no-brainer!

41) Adpost.com. This site gets around 30 million page views per month. It's free to post a basic classified ad, which will run for 30 days – including the possibility of free renewal for up to 90 days.

42) AdLandPro.com. One of the oldest classified ad and community network sites (since 1998), this site also has forums and groups that you can engage with. You can leave comments, with a link to your website or Capture page.

43) ClassifiedsForFree.com. A quick and easy way to reach thousands of people for a relatively small cost. Be relentless in posting classified adverts and watch your referrals GROW!

44) NationwideAdvertising.com. Another useful strategy to add to your marketing plan. Posts your ads to thousands of newspapers for a fee.

45) Local newspaper advertising. We're so focused on things like SEO and content marketing that it's easy to forget about traditional newspaper advertising. Write a GREAT ad, and then send it to a newspaper. Most will design and typeset it for you. Run ads daily: it's so easy and so effective. Always send prospects to your Capture page, and make sure you include your phone number. Give people an option of how to contact you!

Costs usually depend on the average circulation of the paper, the size of the advertisement, and the cost per thousand people 'reading your ad'. Don't miss out on this incredible method.

46) National newspaper advertising. Reach further with national newspaper advertising. You might be wondering if this is really worth it... Yes it is worth it! You'll reach a different market by advertising offline that you'll never reach online.

47) Local magazines. Advertise daily and be RELENTLESS! Advertise with local magazines by grabbing a copy of the latest and contacting them through the listed contact information.

48) Niche magazines. Niche magazines are definitely worth considering as these are thoroughly read and allow you to zero in on your target audience. A great way to gather prospects.

49) Monster.com. As with classified ads sites, job sites can be a

way of building awareness – FAST. Monster is one of the most popular job sites on the Internet. With 17 million unique visitors per month, this is the one you should go for if any.

People who are looking for a job may be open-minded to looking at alternative sources of income. Try posting an advert saying 'Entrepreneurs wanted' with a link to your website; explain what the opportunity is and you may get some referrals into your business.

50) CareerBuilder. CareerBuilder is also one of the most popular job sites, with 24 million unique visitors per month. GET ON IT!

51) Indeed.com. The world's number one job site, with over 180 million unique visitors per month from over 60 different countries. This is definitely one you should consider.

52) Yahoo Pay Per Click (PPC). A great alternative to Google Adwords, with lower costs and competition, the Yahoo! Bing network is another way to get results. As always with PPC, you only pay per click.

Choose keywords that people will search for, like 'make money online', 'financial freedom' or 'work from home', for example. When they search for these keywords, your ad will appear on the page. Simple yet effective.

So what does the cost 'per click' depend on? Well, a variety of factors, such as: the keywords, the maximum amount you've specified you're willing to pay for each click, and your quality score (something that improves over time).

Try to make specific ads for each keyword, and choose a small number of keywords to focus on at first.

53) Google PPC. With Google Adwords, Google revolutionised advertising. With the first entirely measurable advertising platform, the ability to know your exact Return on Investment (ROI) became a possibility. Make the most of Google's search volume and utilise PPC advertising with Google Adwords.

54) Facebook PPC. As social media should be a part of any online marketing campaign, Facebook PPC is a good choice. After all, Facebook has the highest number of monthly active users of any social network in the world. Facebook ads have a global audience, attractive visuals and personalised targeting.

55) BidVertiser. If you'd prefer to go for a dedicated PPC company, BidVertiser is an established ad network that allows you to advertise across thousands of websites. Simply browse the website directory and select those you want, the keywords, geographic targeting, and your PPC bids.

56) Write articles. **Gear them towards your target market and submit them to industry magazines.Content is king; there's no doubt about it. Always include a link to your Capture page.**

57) Guest blogs. **Write guest post on other blogs in your target market. Writing guest posts is another brilliant strategy, because the blogs already have an audience! Offer to write something for other blogs in your target market.**

58) Third-party articles. **Use third-party article sites such as Article City. If you're not confident in your own writing ability, no problem: try sites like Article City to add some free content to your blog.**

59) Search Engine Optimised (SEO) blog posts. **SEO is something you don't want to overlook in today's marketing landscape. Who doesn't want their website to be more visible in search engine results? Use SEO tactics to your advantage by optimising your blog posts with this in mind. Do your research before you use specific keywords and terms. Most importantly, monitor and analyse your traffic regularly.**

60) Cutting Edge Media. **This company specialises in lead generation for network marketing. In other words, you pay for leads. Whilst some leads will be good, others won't – so just keep this in mind if you do decide to pay for leads.**

61) Sales Genie. A similar company, Sales Genie does free trials that last for 3 days and include 150 free leads. AWESOME!

62) ResumeLeads. If you don't fancy posting on job sites, this is an alternative you might like. ResumeLeads.com finds sales candidates and sends them to you via email.

63) SalesLeadsPlus. SalesLeadsPlus.com also offers affordable sales leads. Leads can be expensive so take advantage here.

64) Free eBooks. As I mentioned earlier in the list, providing value is a sure-fire way to get referrals. One of the most popular ways of doing this amongst successful bloggers is to give away free eBooks in return for sign-ups. Although you can write an eBook relatively quickly, you can reap the rewards for much longer. Plus, writing books is great fun – I should know!

65) Free training videos. Another format you can use is video. If you regularly post on a blog, for many topics there is usually some training needed to implement your advice. Provide this too in the form of a video – what problems can you solve for your target audience?

66) Free prize giveaways. This one speaks for itself. Prizes are a great way to facilitate engagement and attract attention. Promote social sharing by offering a prize to one of the people who shares

your post. Or run a competition of sorts. You can get creative with this, and get people engaged in your content in a way other tactics won't.

67) Free lunches. Why should you offer a free lunch? Because you can use it to spread your message – use it as an interactive discussion. Let a paper list go around where people can write down their details. If you get someone to sign up offline, they might be more loyal than those you sign up online!

68) Webinars. Hosting a free webinar is a great way to get yourself an audience. Offer up your time to provide a free training webinar, and watch the referrals roll in! BOOM!

69) Chamber of Commerce. You can use this independent business network to connect with others. Go along to the regular events that will be happening locally and nationally; introduce yourself, ask if people are looking to earn an additional income and hand over one of your business cards! Simple.

70) Job fairs. Job fairs are another way to grow your network. Be prepared, professional and dress the part to make a good impression.

71) Public conventions and conferences. Networking at these kinds of events can a brilliant opportunity to find new referrals.

To stand out from the crowd, don't forget to actually follow up! Just collecting business cards is a waste of time – this is about building long-term relationships.

72) Trade shows. Another cheap, easy way to find referrals. Just remember that you're not actually there to take something away; try and help out others instead. This mentality will take you far as a networker.

73) Colleges. A place many forget to look for networking opportunities. Colleges will often run open days and invite guests and industry specialists. Link in with Business Study courses in particular and you'll be surrounded by young open minds.

74) Industry-specific events. Be proactive and introduce yourself to as many people as you can! Be RELENTLESS!

75) Guru events. Guru events are swarming with people looking for personal-development opportunities. Provide them with one.

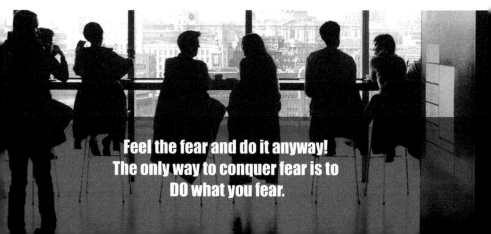

Feel the fear and do it anyway!
The only way to conquer fear is to
DO what you fear.

76) Create a podcast. **Podcasts are a popular medium you WILL want to take advantage of. Provide advice and tips so that people want to come back for more and you'll build a dedicated following.**

77) ListSwapper.com. **Email swap your list with other online marketers. Imagine: you're getting access to so many more prospects all at once. That's what I call a NO-BRAINER. Send them a mailing, a link to a recent blog post or text them with an offer as ONE of your daily actions. Well done SUPERSTAR!**

78) Write press releases. **This can help your business gain valuable PR. Get a feel for the kinds of stories certain publications and programmes already cover until you've got a great story. What's stopping you? Get writing!**

79) Advertise on other YouTube videos. **You don't need to have your own successful channel to get noticed on YouTube. Cut out the hard work and advertise on other videos instead. SIMPLE.**

80) Sponsor other podcasts. **The same goes for podcasts: who says you need your own? You can sponsor others to get the word out there instead.**

81) SoloAdDirectory.com. **Use this directory to buy Solo Ads – these allow you to buy a mailing to another marketer's list. In**

return for an upfront payment, they will promote your offer.

82) Advertise in eNewsletters. A fast way to get your name out there. eNewsletters are one of the easiest and least expensive methods of promoting yourself.

83) Propose Solo Ads to bloggers. As an alternative (or addition) to SoloAdDirectory.com, try contacting popular bloggers directly and see if they'll promote your offer.

84) Solo Ad swaps with other marketers. You can also offer an exchange of Solo Ad promotions with other marketers.

85) Avertise in vacant windows. Put signs in vacant office building windows. Traditional marketing tactics can still go a long way. Many of us tend to look into windows as we walk past, or look at signs if we're hanging around waiting on the street.

86) Telephone hold call message. Put a marketing message on a telephone hold call. If they're on hold they're sure to hear your message!

87) Movie theatre ads. You'll quite literally have an audience.

88) Mobile billboards. Billboards are pretty hard to miss, and research has shown that they really do work. In one study, for

example, 98% of drivers indicated that they noticed mobile billboard ads.

89) Sell and network with the buyers. You don't have to go through traditional avenues to network. Everyone you meet is a potential referral – and these individuals are parting with their cash already.

90) Lorry and truck ads. As well as the side of the road, get your business *on* the road.

91) Bench ads. Benches are everywhere, and so are opportunities for you to get noticed.

92) Bus shelter ads. Who says these are just for big movie releases?

93) Small billboards. Place these around town. As we've established previously, billboards do actually work. Why stick to mobile billboards?

94) Fishbowls. Fishbowls at local restaurants are basically lead boxes. Get a fishbowl, attach a pen and prize slips, and make it look nice. Decide what you'll offer to those willing to leave their information in the fishbowl. This could be a raffle. Collect the fishbowl regularly and contact those who've left their info – many

will choose to leave business cards.

Of course, you should still give someone the prize – this might be a giftcard, for example. But call those who haven't won to say that although they didn't win you'd like to offer them something of significant value.

95) Roadside signs. In addition to billboards, put up smaller signs. They may not be as huge, but roadside signs are more affordable and will allow you to cover more ground.

96) Supermarket checkouts. I bet you haven't thought of this one! Imagine how many people will pick up information at the checkout each day.

97) Restaurant menus. Advertising here is another unique place for lead generation.

98) Shopping trolley ads. As well as check stands, there's also an opportunity to advertise your brand on shopping carts.

99) Yellow Page ads. A well-established local business directory in which advertising is an easy, affordable option.

100) Window lettering on vehicles. If some simple lettering will do the trick, get your name up on the windows of vehicles.

101) Trade show booths. In addition to attending trade shows, why not get a booth up? This is a great way of providing more information and allows you to network at the same time.

102) Taxi signs. Get in touch with a local firm to get your brand on show – on something people actually look for.

103) Mail postcard. For those in favour of a more direct approach, a direct mail postcard campaign might be for you.

104) Mail coupon books. People love free stuff. As an alternative to a postcard campaign, try a coupon book instead.

105) Website Search Engine Optimisation (SEO). Its importance today cannot be underestimated. SEO tactics have worked and still work for me. Get implementing SEO tips on your website.

106) Referrals. Another one for those of you who prefer a more direct approach. Simply ask for referrals! Do you know anyone who would be interested in your product/services/ opportunity? And do you know who they know? If you don't ask, you won't get.

107) Network at related clubs and organisations. Lead-generation is all about meeting like-minded people. One of the best places to do just that is at clubs and organisations.

108) Marketing materials into invoices and bills. **This is an ideal opportunity to include several of your drop cards. The reason being? When your recipient opens the envelope, they will likely have colleagues in the office with them, and they will hand your information around! You're a marketing ROCKSTAR!**

109) Kiosks in shopping centres. **In addition to trade show booths, shopping centres and malls are another place you can put up kiosks.**

110) Host a Cashflow 101 Club. **If you've not heard of Robert Kiyosaki, you need to familiarise yourself with him. This investor and self-help author created the Cashflow 101 game to reinforce the information in his books. This is a great way to learn financial strategies and accounting principles. Hosting your own club is a great way to meet like-minded individuals.**

111) Sponsor charity events. **All for a good cause and gets your name out there. What could be better?**

112) Write an article in a local publication. **Get in front of someone else's audience by writing something in a local publication.**

113) Become a speaker. **Speaking at an event or a conference is a great way to make a lasting impression. You'll have the**

audience's attention for a much longer time and they'll get to know, like and TRUST you. A PHENOMENAL way to build your personal brand.

114) Organise an event. Find a great location that is close to a train station or motorway. Set a date, create an event on Facebook and invite EVERYONE you know. Give a presentation on a topic you know about and give people lots of opporuntity to network. But be sure to promote it RELENTLESSLY.

115) Joint ventures. Why not pool your resources? You can share leads and grow your list. Contact one new person a day.

116) Send messages on LinkedIn. LinkedIn is an effective way to connect with professionals. You can also ask someone else in your network to introduce you to a particular person if you need to.

117) Facebook groups targeted to your niche. In addition to connecting with individuals directly, try creating a group or fan page targeted to your niche. This can be an effective way of discovering new leads if existing members invite others to join too. Be sure to post in five groups daily for one of your actions.

118) Sponsored posts on Facebook. Facebook is known for its highly-targeted marketing tactics. Get your business up on the sponsored posts to get seen.

119) Reverse marketing in Facebook groups. Reverse marketing involves encouraging people to seek your business out on their own. Provide valuable info in Facebook groups, without actually asking them to 'buy' or 'commit' to anything, and they will come to you. Google 'reverse marketing' for more info.

120) Reverse marketing with Google. You can also do the same thing on Google. And we all know how powerful that is!

121) Sell to the sellers! When you get a phone call from a cold caller or salesperson, share your opportunity with them in return. It's cheeky, but you just never know...

122) Write an advertorial. Magazine and newspaper editors LOVE receiving well-written content from contributing authors – it makes the job of filling up their publication easier. Advertorials differ from usual articles in that they allow you to actively promote your opportunity. Be sure to write content that is useful and relevant to the readership – address a problem or concern they have and then show them how you can help! YOU ARE A ROCKSTAR!

123) Target people on Twitter. Follow 30 TARGETED people on Twitter. 30 follows equals ONE of your daily tasks. I want you to also directly message the people you follow and ask, 'Do you keep your options open?' This is the question I was asked that HOOKED me into Direct Sales all those years ago. GENIUS!

124) Pitch to anyone, anywhere. Take advantage of those moments when you're already stood or sat with someone for a period of time. Ask them about their work, their life. Listen to their answers. At the right time, ask them if they're open-minded to new opportunities. Give them your business card and ask them to take a look at your website and sign up for more information.

125) Collect testimonials. There aren't many things that work better for promoting your business than a good testimonial – even better if you can capture it on video. Ask a happy customer to share with you how your business or opportunity has transformed their life and then share it on all of The Big 7 social media accounts.

126) Special offers or discounts. People love to feel that they're getting a bargain. Send out an offer or discount with a time limit on it using any of your social media accounts or by email.

127) Traditional mailings. Remember those? Posters on car windows or through letterboxes? Since the Internet came along they may be considered old-school, but they can still work a dream – so make this one of your 3–5 actions and see the results!

128) Use Google Local. People still use this to search for local business, and it's FREE. It will also help with your Search Engine Optimisation, so it's definitely worth setting up an account.

129) Facebook Live! This is HUGELY impressive and current. Think about it: if you just get 100 people looking at your Live video, it's like presenting your offer to 100 people in a room. Do this daily, and watch your referrals go through the ROOF! At the end of the video, be sure to add a 'Call to Action', such as:

'I'm looking for two new people to join my business and I invite you to take a serious look'. Let them have your website address or Capture page and then say, 'The first two people to join me will get a free copy of my eBook'. Give them an incentive and a deadline. BOOM. YOU'RE IN!!

130) Post in Facebook groups. Identify and join TARGETED Facebook groups. Post a link to a relevant blog in AT LEAST five groups. Ask people to leave you a comment. Five posts equals one action.

In this book I've provided you with 130 marketing tips, but of course there are many, MANY more ways to promote your business. If you want to use other methods and do more, then my advice is **ALWAYS DO MORE!**

FREE 100+ MARKETING TIPS

Summary of marketing tips:

1. Pick up the phone
2. Advertise on bank notes
3. Facebook videos
4. Blog
5. Promote your blog
6. Join LinkedIn groups
7. Leave drop cards
8. Tweet your blog
9. Instagram
10. YouTube videos
11. Comment on blogs
12. Comment on YouTube videos
13. Freebies
14. Easy hits
15. Text marketing
16. Email your list daily
17. Advertise on the back window of your car
18. eBay advertising
19. Advertise in shop windows
20. Notice boards
21. Roadside ads
22. About.me
23. WhatsApp
24. Skype marketing
25. Fiverr.com
26. Target your niche
27. BuySellAds.com
28. ClixSense.com
29. NeoBux.com
30. WarriorForum.com
31. BigAdvertising.co.uk
32. SoloAdGuru.com
33. Advertise on your car number plate
34. Snapchat
35. Coffee meetings
36. Craigslist.com
37. Backpage.com

38. Gumtree.com
39. Oodle.com
40. ClassifiedAds.com
41. Adpost.com
42. AdLandPro.com
43. ClassifiedsForFree.com
44. NationwideAdvertising.com
45. Local newspaper advertising
46. National newspaper advertising
47. Local magazines
48. Niche magazines
49. Monster.com
50. CareerBuilder
51. Indeed.com
52. Yahoo Pay Per Click
53. Google PPC
54. Facebook PPC
55. BidVertiser
56. Write articles
57. Guest blogs
58. Third-party articles
59. SEO in your blog posts
60. Cutting Edge Media
61. Sales Genie
62. Resume Leads
63. Sales Leads Plus
64. Free eBooks
65. Free training videos
66. Free prize giveaways
67. Free lunches
68. Webinars
69. Chamber of Commerce
70. Job fairs
71. Public conventions and conferences
72. Trade shows
73. Colleges
74. Industry-specific events
75. Guru events

76. Create a podcast
77. ListSwapper.com
78. Write press releases
79. Advertise on other YouTube videos
80. Sponsor other podcasts
81. Buy solo ads on SoloAdDirectory. com
82. Advertise in eNewsletters
83. Propose Solo Ads to bloggers
84. Solo Ad swaps with other marketers
85. Advertise in vacant windows
86. Telephone hold call message
87. Movie theatre ads
88. Mobile billboard
89. Sell and network with buyers
90. Lorry and truck ads
91. Bench ads
92. Bus shelter ads
93. Small billboards
94. Fishbowls
95. Roadside signs
96. Supermarket checkouts
97. Restaurant menus
98. Shopping trolley ads
99. Yellow Page ads
100. Window lettering on vehicles
101. Trade show booth
102. Taxi signs
103. Mail postcard
104. Mail coupon books
105. Website SEO

106. Referrals
107. Network at related clubs and organisations
108. Marketing materials into invoices and bills
109. Kiosks in shopping centres
110. Host a Cashflow 101 Club
111. Sponsor charity events
112. Write an article for a local publication
113. Become a speaker
114. Organise an event
115. Joint ventures
116. Send messages on LinkedIn
117. Facebook groups targeted for your niche
118. Sponsored posts on Facebook
119. Reverse marketing with Facebook groups
120. Reverse marketing with Google
121. Sell to the sellers!
122. Write an advertorial
123. Target people on Twitter
124. Pitch to anyone, anywhere
125. Collect testimonials
126. Special offers or discounts
127. Traditional mailings
128. Use Google Local
129. Facebook live videos
130. Post in Facebook groups

I've personally sponsored 5000+ direct referrals in just over two and a half years by taking these actions and teaching my team to do the same. And this is just in one business. In my previous business, I personally sponsored 1000+ active referrals. Consistency is key.

Be relentless, be focused, be **ADDICTED!** Be ferocious, and teach your team to be the same. Work like you're poor. Find your passion and help others.

Chapter 6

YOUR 90 DAY CHALLENGE

📅

Keep away from people who try
to belittle your ambitions. Small
people always do that, but the
really great make you feel that
you too can become great

~ Mark Twain ~

Introducing The 90 Day Challenge

ARE YOU READY??!!! Because before you begin to complete the Action Tracker, you need to absolutely commit yourself for the next 90 days. If you miss a day, I'm going to be asking you to start right back from Day 1. It is VITAL that you complete 90 consecutive days: no ducking out, no excuses. This plan only works if you take action 90 days in a row.

Saying that, I understand that there may be days when you absolutely can't complete your actions – for example if you're genuinely sick then you need to rest and get back to good heath. There are rare situations when this happens, when 'life' just gets in the way. However, a family wedding isn't one of those situations. Get up an hour earlier and complete your actions before you go. Plan your day. It takes five minutes to record and upload a video, even less to post a Tweet. Minutes to make a call. Having a social life or attending a family gathering does not excuse you from your commitments.

Imagine heading off to your event knowing that you've done what you need to do in order to build your business. You'll feel great!

Now imagine going out for the day only hoping that you'll make more money. Let me tell you this: it isn't going to happen unless you put the work in.

You need to COMMIT and take ACTION every day

Think for a moment about the power of this plan. Take one of the actions as an example… Let's say that for 90 consecutive days you post a video onto YouTube about your business. That's 90 videos out there!! And then imagine if you got your team doing the same thing – you'll be flooding the Internet with information about your business. This is how billion-dollar companies are made. The potential is MASSIVE! **It's PHENOMENAL!!**

Remember: posting a YouTube video is only one of your 3–5 tasks. In the same timeframe, you could have also posted the same amount of videos onto Facebook. And that's just two tasks per day. You could have also spoken to 90 new people over the same 90-day period. That's 90 people who now know about your business who didn't before. And think about all of the people they could be telling! Three simple and easy actions, and all that exposure for your business, in about 10 minutes a day!

Let's take this a step further...

Imagine you have a team of 10 people working the plan for 90 days. If you teach this plan to 10 people, all of a sudden your organisation is speaking to 900 new people, and so this means there are 900 videos going out there, not 90. This is huge! Consider what this would do to your organisation. It's mind-blowing. It's going to EXPLODE your business.

THE POWER OF DUPLICATION

The Power of TEN People

Imagine you have a team of TEN people with a copy of this book, working the plan for 90 days. Let's say that you all decide to do one video each on YouTube for the duration of the plan. In just one day, you'll have TEN new videos out there on YouTube alone. Now, get everyone to put that same video on Facebook, and immediately you have the same number of videos going out on Facebook too! In addition, let's say you each talk to one new person each day: you're talking to 10 new people about your business INSTANTLY. You also decide to each do a blog post and place a classified ad; all of a sudden you have TEN new blog posts out, as well as TEN classified ads.

This is where the REAL POWER is

With just TEN of you taking ACTION for 90 days in a row, you'll have 900 videos on YouTube, you'll have 900 videos on Facebook, you'll have talked to 900 new people, placed 900 classified ads and you'll have 900 blog posts out there. Now that's HUGE. ALL about your business. Now, if this isn't going to double your income and business in 90 days, nothing ever will.

This will EXPLODE your business, and we're only talking a small number of people. I'm going to take it a step further and show you what happens when you have 100 people in your team doing this...

THE POWER OF DUPLICATION

The Power of ONE HUNDRED People

Are you sitting down? This is EVEN MORE powerful!

Here's what happens when you have 100 people in your team – with a copy of this book – doing this Daily Plan of Action for 90 days in a row:

9000 videos on YouTube – WOW!
9000 videos on Facebook – THATS MENTAL!
9000 blog posts – INSANE!
9000 classified ads – MASSIVE!
AND your team will have talked to 9000 new people about your business – WOW, THAT'S AMAZING!

Not only that, but these videos, and blog posts will continue to get you traffic. The people you speak to will speak to people they know. The growth will be UNSTOPPABLE. WOW!

As you can see, this is going to MORE THAN DOUBLE your business. Take action NOW, get started TODAY!

This is how you build empires! This is powerful stuff!

THE POWER OF DUPLICATION

The Power of ONE THOUSAND People

You'd better be sitting down again for this…

You've been doing The 90 Day Challenge for several months. EVERYONE in your organisation has a copy of this book, and 1000 people are ACTIVELY doing their 3–5 tasks each day. That's 1000 people putting a video out there each day on YouTube, 1000 videos on Facebook and so on. WOW! That's what you call flooding the market!

But here's where the magic happens! In 90 days this is:

90,000 videos on YouTube about your business – INSANE!
90,000 videos on Facebook – PHENOMENAL!
90,000 blog posts – MIND-BLOWING!
90,000 classified ads about your business – WHOOOOA!
AND 90,000 new people spoken to – SPEECHLESS!

Do you think there will be some sponsorship? A difference to your business? You're going to be a household name! And this is easy to do, because remember: you're only doing 3–5 actions and your team is doing the rest. Imagine this! WOW!

All you need to do is make sure your team get copies of this amazing book – all of them. Make sure they complete The 90 Day Challenge for 90 consecutive days. Get them to show you their completed daily task sheets.

Anyone who doesn't come to you with it filled in, get them to review their 'Why', because clearly it isn't big enough to drive them to work.

For the people who consistently put the plan into action, you could actually give them some reward and recognition for doing so – whether that's more copies of this book to hand out to their own teams, or something else you know will continue to inspire them.

As we've seen, 100 people taking action will make a MASSIVE difference. 1000 people is ENORMOUS growth. This is why I HIGHLY recommend that you invest in multiple copies of this book – 5, 10 or 100+ copies at a time – and give them out to your team members. Coach them to invest in copies and hand them out too. I can assure you this is a small investment in your business that will explode your income to another level. You will see MORE THAN a return on investment if you follow this advice to the letter.

Believe me... this plan will absolutely EXPLODE your business.

WOW. This is staggering. NOW it's making sense; NOW you're feeling the power!

With The 90 Day Challenge, you can MORE THAN double your business in 90 days!

Do not underestimate the power of this plan

Remember to keep asking yourself; why are you doing this? Keep motivated! Is it because you want that Rolls Royce? Do you want it bad enough to stay motivated? If you don't, you need to review and change your goals. Your goals need to get you leaping out of bed each day!

I urge you to work through your actions in the mornings if you can. Don't leave it until 11.55pm in the evening. Even though it's still do-able at that time of day (you can do a Tweet, post a 30-second video onto YouTube and Facebook, or call someone in a different part of the world). Think about the message you're sending to yourself if you leave the most important part of your work until last thing at night. Bring it into the forefront of your life, focus on it, prioritise it, TAKE ACTION and you will be rewarded.

I want you to delete all of your excuses RIGHT NOW!

We're not far from getting to work. This book holds you accountable to yourself, to your commitment to your goals, vision and dreams. As you explore the Action Tracker, you'll see that not only do you need to tick a box to say that you've completed your 3–5 actions each day, but that I want you to record exactly what those actions were. I've provided a completed planner as a demonstration, to help you get started. USE IT!

Recording your actions in this way is powerful. It means you can look back and see your activity over a whole 90 days. Not only that, but you can look back and review your actions and see what was successful. This helps you to review your activities and make decisions about how to best use your energy in the future. That's business intelligence!

So let's get going with The 90 Day Challenge. Three is my recommended minimum, but the Action Tracker has the space for up to five – and it goes without saying that five is better. People tend do what you do and so if you do the minimum, your team will tend do the minimum also. I coach all of my team to do at least five actions per day, if not more... Something you'll learn more about later in the book.

Once you begin to see how you can DOUBLE your business in such a short space of time, I can guarantee that you're not going to want to stop. And once you've fully completed the Action Tracker in this book, invest in another copy to start all over again!

Invest in more copies at: The90DayChallenge.biz

Want to know the BEST way to build your business?

Invest in 5, 10 or even 100+ copies of this book and get all of your team to do the same.

Imagine the power and the income you can generate if ALL of your team are following the same plan.

This will EXPLODE your business.

Take action NOW and order your copies here:

The90DayChallenge.biz

YOU <u>CAN</u> DOUBLE YOUR BUSINESS AND INCOME IN 90 DAYS!

~ SIMON STEPSYS ~

The Active and Passive approaches

We talked a little earlier about this, but I want to return to it for a moment. You're going to be reaching out in a minimum of three – but ideally five – ways each day that will build your business.

Most people in Direct Sales fail because they are only using the Passive approaches, and so their sponsorship remains low. With the Passive approach, they are putting out a video or messaging their list, and hoping that people will respond and join the business. They all want to be Attraction Marketers, and whilst there are people out there who are great at this, it takes time to build up your personal brand and awareness via this route. If you're going to take only Passive actions, I can't promise that you'll double your business in 90 days. Again, if you do one Active marketing action each day – by directly approaching a new prospect – then in my mind you will absolutely double your business in 90 days.

What is Active Marketing?

Active Marketing is picking up the phone and proactively pursuing someone to join your business. Or, it's Actively direct messaging someone with a view to recruiting them into your business.

Of your 3–5 daily actions, I highly advise that AT LEAST ONE is Active Marketing. Better still, if you can talk to five new people each day for 90 days, you can forget about doubling your income; you can quadruple it and more! Pick up the phone and you're in business BIG TIME!

A quick recap

Remember; three actions is the minimum I recommend: ideally I want you to be doing five. This is for your benefit, but also, your team will follow your lead. And so if you do five tasks a day, they will too. Is that going to make a difference to your business? Absolutely.

Think about it like this. If you alone complete three tasks for 90 days, you'll have done 270 tasks. However, five tasks for 90 days is 450 tasks! That's INSANE!

Now imagine you have 10 of your team doing this, that's 2700 tasks based on just three actions daily, and... a WHOPPING 4500 tasks if you do five actions!

You're almost doubling your activity by taking five actions. So aim for five tasks daily. In fact, do as I do: do a **minimum** of five. On an average day, I do more than five, and even when time is short I still do five as my daily MINIMUM!

Of course, if you want to do more, then do more! But be aware, if you decide to do seven actions in one day, this doesn't mean you can do fewer the next!

BE RELENTLESSLY ADDICTED to your daily actions.

MOTIVATION GETS YOU STARTED, HABIT KEEPS IT GOING!

~ Jim Rohn ~

YOUR 90 DAY CHALLENGE

Stay FOCUSED! Reach out in at least 3 – 5 ways DAILY, complete the boxes below and put a TICK in the circle when you've done your actions for the day!

DAY No.	**1**	**2**	**3**	**4**	**5**
1	Spoke to new prospect J. Smith on phone	Wrote 500 word Blog + Posted to 5 FB Groups	Spoke to P. Jones on phone - new referral	Sent TEXT offer to all contacts	Posted in 5 target Facebook Groups
2	Placed Ad on Craiglist	Called new Prospect J Bloggs	Went out - left 30 dropcards		
3	Created & Posted video on YouTube	Followed 30 people on Twitter & Msg them directly	Phoned new Prospect Louise Smith	Facebook Live video about business	
4	500 word Blog - posted in FB Groups	Put out 30 drop cards			
1	Emailed list with time limited offer	Hosted a free Live Webinar 87 people viewed	Placed 5 Ads on NeoBux. com	Messaged 30 people on Snapchat directly	Hosted a coffee mtg with 20 prospects

AN EXAMPLE OF A COMPLETED TRACKER

REACH OUT IN AT LEAST 3–5 WAYS DAILY!!

DAY 1: Amazing start! Well done – you achieved 5 out of 5 and took an ACTIVE action today. You gave it the full monty! Kerrrching!

DAY 2: AWESOME!! 3 out of 5 keeps you on track, LOVE THIS! Keep it going!

DAY 3: Well done. You achieved 4 actions today, and made a direct contact with a potential new client! YOU ROCK!

DAY 4: Whoooaaa!! What went wrong? Whilst you achieved 2 actions today, you didn't hit your minimum of 3. :-(sorry but you've got to go back to Day 1 and restart The 90 Day Challenge. Remember it's about forming new habits... so keep on top of those daily actions and those habits will become effortless.

DAY 1: Life happens; forgive yourself and start again but consider this... Is your WHY strong enough?
Keep going – keep on doing at least 3 actions a day

How bad do you want it?

Are you doing the minimum of **THREE** actions or are you doing **FIVE?**

Be like me: I do **FIVE** every day without evening thinking about it. And of course remember this: if you do the minimum your team will do the minimum. If you do the FIVE, so will your team. So keep asking yourself, 'How badly do I want it?'

Those who know me, know how driven I am; but those of you who don't know me won't. FIVE tasks per day is not a huge amount but it will make a MASSIVE difference.

TIME HAS MORE VALUE THAN MONEY!

~ Simon Stepsys ~

LET'S NOT WASTE ANOTHER MOMENT – LET'S GET TO WORK ...

Stay FOCUSED! Reach out in at least 3–5 ways
DAILY, complete the boxes below and put a TICK in
the circle when you've done your actions for the day!

90 DAY CHALLENGE!

Y

1	2	3	4	5

ANYONE CAN BE
A MILLIONAIRE
IF THEY WANT IT
BAD ENOUGH

SIMON STEPSYS

Stay FOCUSED! Reach out in at least 3–5 ways
DAILY, complete the boxes below and put a TICK in
the circle when you've done your actions for the day!

90 DAY CHALLENGE!

DAY	1	2	3	4	5	
○						○
○						○
○						○
○						○
○						○
○						○
○						○

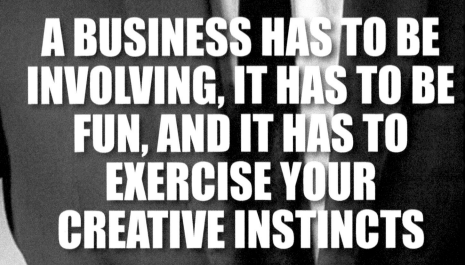

A BUSINESS HAS TO BE INVOLVING, IT HAS TO BE FUN, AND IT HAS TO EXERCISE YOUR CREATIVE INSTINCTS

SIMON STEPSYS

Stay FOCUSED! Reach out in at least 3–5 ways DAILY, complete the boxes below and put a TICK in the circle when you've done your actions for the day!

90 DAY CHALLENGE!

DAY	1	2	3	4	5	
						○
						○
						○
						○
						○
						○
						○

STAY POSITIVE,
WORK HARD,
MAKE IT HAPPEN

SIMON STEPSYS

90 DAY CHALLENGE!

Stay FOCUSED! Reach out in at least 3–5 ways DAILY, complete the boxes below and put a TICK in the circle when you've done your actions for the day!

Y	1	2	3	4	5

SET AN EXAMPLE TO YOUR TEAM

The speed of the leader = the speed of the team!

SIMON STEPSYS

Over $3.8 million in earnings and 5,000 PLUS direct referrals in 29 months! And you can do this too!

Stay FOCUSED! Reach out in at least 3–5 ways DAILY, complete the boxes below and put a TICK in the circle when you've done your actions for the day!

90 DAY CHALLENGE!

	1	2	3	4	5
Y					

SURROUND YOURSELF WITH WINNERS

SIMON STEPSYS

Stay FOCUSED! Reach out in at least 3–5 ways DAILY, complete the boxes below and put a TICK in the circle when you've done your actions for the day!

90 DAY CHALLENGE!

DAY

1	2	3	4	5

DO SOMETHING YOU LOVE EACH DAY

SIMON STEPSYS

Stay FOCUSED! Reach out in at least 3–5 ways DAILY, complete the boxes below and put a TICK in the circle when you've done your actions for the day!

90 DAY CHALLENGE!

Y | **1** | **2** | **3** | **4** | **5**

MASSIVE
ACTION = MASSIVE
RESULTS!

Little Action = Little Result (if any!)

~Simon Stepsys~

Stay FOCUSED! Reach out in at least 3–5 ways
DAILY, complete the boxes below and put a TICK in
the circle when you've done your actions for the day!

90 DAY CHALLENGE!

Y	1	2	3	4	5

THE SKY WAS
NEVER THE
LIMIT

SIMON STEPSYS

Stay FOCUSED! Reach out in at least 3–5 ways
DAILY, complete the boxes below and put a TICK in
the circle when you've done your actions for the day!

90 DAY CHALLENGE!

Y	**1**	**2**	**3**	**4**	**5**

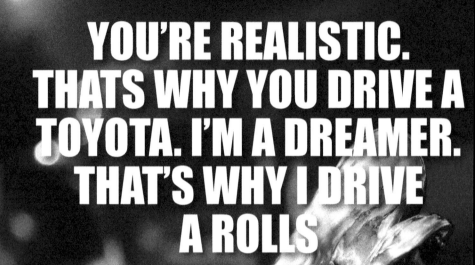

YOU'RE REALISTIC. THATS WHY YOU DRIVE A TOYOTA. I'M A DREAMER. THAT'S WHY I DRIVE A ROLLS

SIMON STEPSYS

Stay FOCUSED! Reach out in at least 3–5 ways
DAILY, complete the boxes below and put a TICK in
the circle when you've done your actions for the day!

90 DAY CHALLENGE!

Y

1	2	3	4	5

STOP COMPLAINING ABOUT YOUR CIRCUMSTANCES. DO SOMETHING ABOUT IT

SIMON STEPSYS

Stay FOCUSED! Reach out in at least 3–5 ways DAILY, complete the boxes below and put a TICK in the circle when you've done your actions for the day!

90 DAY CHALLENGE!

	1	2	3	4	5

YOUR MIND MUST ARRIVE AT A DESTINATION BEFORE YOU DO

SIMON STEPSYS

Stay FOCUSED! Reach out in at least 3–5 ways
DAILY, complete the boxes below and put a TICK in
the circle when you've done your actions for the day!

90 DAY CHALLENGE!

DAY	1	2	3	4	5	
						○
						○
						○
						○
						○
						○
						○

IF YOU'RE TIRED OF STARTING OVER, STOP GIVING UP

SIMON STEPSYS

Stay FOCUSED! Reach out in at least 3–5 ways
DAILY, complete the boxes below and put a TICK in
the circle when you've done your actions for the day!

90 DAY CHALLENGE!

Y

1	2	3	4	5

DON'T EVER GO WITH THE FLOW. BE THE FLOW

SIMON STEPSYS

Stay FOCUSED! Reach out in at least 3–5 ways DAILY, complete the boxes below and put a TICK in the circle when you've done your actions for the day!

90 DAY CHALLENGE!

DAY	1	2	3	4	5	
						○
						○
						○
						○
						○
						○
						○

BE SO FINANCIALLY SECURE THAT YOU FORGET IT'S PAYDAY

SIMON STEPSYS

Stay FOCUSED! Reach out in at least 3–5 ways
DAILY, complete the boxes below and put a TICK in
the circle when you've done your actions for the day!

90 DAY CHALLENGE!

Y

1	2	3	4	5

WORK UNTIL EXPENSIVE BECOMES CHEAP

SIMON STEPSYS

Stay FOCUSED! Reach out in at least 3–5 ways DAILY, complete the boxes below and put a TICK in the circle when you've done your actions for the day!

90 DAY CHALLENGE!

DAY	1	2	3	4	5

Stay FOCUSED! Reach out in at least 3–5 ways
DAILY, complete the boxes below and put a TICK in
the circle when you've done your actions for the day!

90 DAY CHALLENGE!

Y	1	2	3	4	5

Stay FOCUSED! Reach out in at least 3–5 ways
DAILY, complete the boxes below and put a TICK in
the circle when you've done your actions for the day!

90 DAY CHALLENGE!

Y

1 **2** **3** **4** **5**

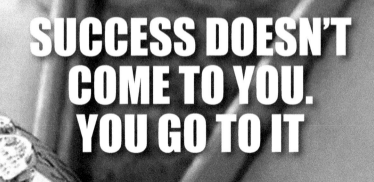

SUCCESS DOESN'T COME TO YOU. YOU GO TO IT

SIMON STEPSYS

Stay FOCUSED! Reach out in at least 3–5 ways DAILY, complete the boxes below and put a TICK in the circle when you've done your actions for the day!

Y	1	2	3	4	5	
						○
						○
						○
						○
						○
						○
						○

Stay FOCUSED! Reach out in at least 3–5 ways DAILY, complete the boxes below and put a TICK in the circle when you've done your actions for the day!

90 DAY CHALLENGE!

Y	1	2	3	4	5
○						○
○						○
○						○
○						○
○						○
○						○
○						○

SUCCESS OCCURS WHEN OPPORTUNITY MEETS PREPERATION

SIMON STEPSYS

Stay FOCUSED! Reach out in at least 3–5 ways DAILY, complete the boxes below and put a TICK in the circle when you've done your actions for the day!

	1	**2**	**3**	**4**	**5**

5AM:
THE HOUR WHEN LEGENDS ARE WAKING UP OR GOING TO SLEEP

SIMON STEPSYS

90 DAY CHALLENGE!

Stay FOCUSED! Reach out in at least 3–5 ways DAILY, complete the boxes below and put a TICK in the circle when you've done your actions for the day!

DAY	1	2	3	4	5	
◯						◯
◯						◯
◯						◯
◯						◯
◯						◯
◯						◯
◯						◯

I'M NOT OBESSED BY MONEY. I'M OBESSED BY FREEDOM

Stay FOCUSED! Reach out in at least 3–5 ways
DAILY, complete the boxes below and put a TICK in
the circle when you've done your actions for the day!

90 DAY CHALLENGE!

1	2	3	4	5

NEVER WORK
FOR PAPER

SIMON STEPSYS

Stay FOCUSED! Reach out in at least 3–5 ways DAILY, complete the boxes below and put a TICK in the circle when you've done your actions for the day!

90 DAY CHALLENGE!

DAY	1	2	3	4	5	
⟍						◯
⟍						◯
⟍						◯
⟍						◯
⟍						◯
⟍						◯
⟍						◯

YOU'VE GOT 2 OPTIONS:
BE BROKE OR
GET MONEY

SIMON STEPSYS

Stay FOCUSED! Reach out in at least 3–5 ways DAILY, complete the boxes below and put a TICK in the circle when you've done your actions for the day!

90 DAY CHALLENGE!

1	2	3	4	5

EITHER YOU RUN THE DAY OR THE DAY RUNS YOU

SIMON STEPSYS

Stay FOCUSED! Reach out in at least 3–5 ways DAILY, complete the boxes below and put a TICK in the circle when you've done your actions for the day!

90 DAY CHALLENGE!

Y	1	2	3	4	5

MONEY
NEVER
SLEEPS

SIMON STEPSYS

Stay FOCUSED! Reach out in at least 3–5 ways
DAILY, complete the boxes below and put a TICK in
the circle when you've done your actions for the day!

90 DAY CHALLENGE!

	1	2	3	4	5

IF YOU WANT TO
ACHIEVE GREATNESS
STOP ASKING
FOR PERMISSION

SIMON STEPSYS

Stay FOCUSED! Reach out in at least 3–5 ways
DAILY, complete the boxes below and put a TICK in
the circle when you've done your actions for the day!

90 DAY CHALLENGE!

Y	**1**	**2**	**3**	**4**	**5**

IF YOU DON'T LEARN HOW TO GET PAID WHILST YOU'RE ASLEEP YOU WILL WORK UNTIL YOU DIE

SIMON STEPS

Stay FOCUSED! Reach out in at least 3–5 ways DAILY, complete the boxes below and put a TICK in the circle when you've done your actions for the day!

90 DAY CHALLENGE!

1	2	3	4	5

Stay FOCUSED! Reach out in at least 3–5 ways DAILY, complete the boxes below and put a TICK in the circle when you've done your actions for the day!

Y	1	2	3	4	5

STOP TRYING TO FIT IN WHEN YOU WERE BORN TO STAND OUT

SIMON STEPSYS

Stay FOCUSED! Reach out in at least 3–5 ways
DAILY, complete the boxes below and put a TICK in
the circle when you've done your actions for the day!

90 DAY CHALLENGE!

1	2	3	4	5

SUCCESSFUL PEOPLE ARE NOT GIFTED. THEY JUST WORK HARD THEN SUCCEED ON PURPOSE

SIMON STEPSYS

Stay FOCUSED! Reach out in at least 3–5 ways
DAILY, complete the boxes below and put a TICK in
the circle when you've done your actions for the day!

90 DAY CHALLENGE!

Y

1	2	3	4	5

IT CAN BE DONE BUT YOU HAVE TO MAKE IT HAPPEN

SIMON STEPSYS

Stay FOCUSED! Reach out in at least 3–5 ways DAILY, complete the boxes below and put a TICK in the circle when you've done your actions for the day!

90 DAY CHALLENGE!

1	2	3	4	5

LIMITS EXIST ONLY IN THE MIND

SIMON STEPSYS

Stay FOCUSED! Reach out in at least 3–5 ways DAILY, complete the boxes below and put a TICK in the circle when you've done your actions for the day!

Y	1	2	3	4	5

BUILD AN EMPIRE WITH THE SAME BRICKS THAT WERE THROWN AT YOU

SIMON STEPSYS

Stay FOCUSED! Reach out in at least 3–5 ways
DAILY, complete the boxes below and put a TICK in
the circle when you've done your actions for the day!

90 DAY CHALLENGE!

	1	2	3	4	5	
						○
						○
						○
						○
						○
						○
						○

SOME DREAM
FOR IT
I WORK FOR IT

SIMON STEPSYS

Stay FOCUSED! Reach out in at least 3–5 ways
DAILY, complete the boxes below and put a TICK in
the circle when you've done your actions for the day!

90 DAY CHALLENGE!

Y	1	2	3	4	5

ALWAYS DO
WHAT YOU ARE
AFRAID TO DO

SIMON STEPSYS

Stay FOCUSED! Reach out in at least 3–5 ways DAILY, complete the boxes below and put a TICK in the circle when you've done your actions for the day!

90 DAY CHALLENGE!

1	2	3	4	5

WORK UNTIL YOU NO LONGER HAVE TO INTRODUCE YOURSELF

SIMON STEPSYS

Stay FOCUSED! Reach out in at least 3–5 ways
DAILY, complete the boxes below and put a TICK in
the circle when you've done your actions for the day!

90 DAY CHALLENGE!

Y	1	2	3	4	5

BELIEVE WHILE OTHERS ARE DOUBTING

SIMON STEPSYS

Stay FOCUSED! Reach out in at least 3–5 ways
DAILY, complete the boxes below and put a TICK in
the circle when you've done your actions for the day!

90 DAY CHALLENGE!

	1	2	3	4	5

Stay FOCUSED! Reach out in at least 3–5 ways DAILY, complete the boxes below and put a TICK in the circle when you've done your actions for the day!

DAY

1	2	3	4	5

DOUBT KILLS MORE DREAMS THAN FAILURE EVER WILL

SIMON STEPSYS

Stay FOCUSED! Reach out in at least 3–5 ways
DAILY, complete the boxes below and put a TICK in
the circle when you've done your actions for the day!

90 DAY CHALLENGE!

	1	**2**	**3**	**4**	**5**

COMFORT ZONES:
WHERE DREAMS
GO TO DIE

SIMON STEPSYS

Stay FOCUSED! Reach out in at least 3–5 ways DAILY, complete the boxes below and put a TICK in the circle when you've done your actions for the day!

Y	1	2	3	4	5

PRESSURE
MAKES
DIAMONDS

SIMON STEPSYS

Stay FOCUSED! Reach out in at least 3–5 ways
DAILY, complete the boxes below and put a TICK in
the circle when you've done your actions for the day!

90 DAY CHALLENGE!

1	2	3	4	5

MOTIVATED BY THE FEAR OF MEDIOCRITY

SIMON STEPSYS

Stay FOCUSED! Reach out in at least 3–5 ways DAILY, complete the boxes below and put a TICK in the circle when you've done your actions for the day!

DAY	**1**	**2**	**3**	**4**	**5**	
◯						◯
◯						◯
◯						◯
◯						◯
◯						◯
◯						◯
◯						◯

IF YOU'RE PERSISTENT YOU WILL GET IT. IF YOU'RE CONSISTENT YOU WILL KEEP IT

SIMON STEPSYS

Stay FOCUSED! Reach out in at least 3–5 ways DAILY, complete the boxes below and put a TICK in the circle when you've done your actions for the day!

90 DAY CHALLENGE!

1	2	3	4	5

DON'T BE AFRAID TO FAIL; BE AFRAID NOT TO TRY

SIMON STEPSYS

Stay FOCUSED! Reach out in at least 3–5 ways DAILY, complete the boxes below and put a TICK in the circle when you've done your actions for the day!

Y	1	2	3	4	5

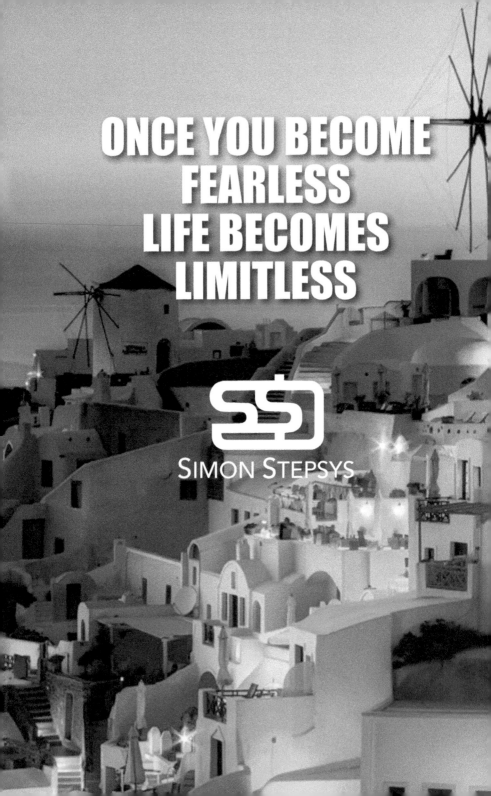

Stay FOCUSED! Reach out in at least 3–5 ways
DAILY, complete the boxes below and put a TICK in
the circle when you've done your actions for the day!

90 DAY CHALLENGE!

1	2	3	4	5

THE ODDS ARE ALL IN MY FAVOUR BECAUSE I NEVER QUIT

SIMON STEPSYS

Stay FOCUSED! Reach out in at least 3–5 ways
DAILY, complete the boxes below and put a TICK in
the circle when you've done your actions for the day!

90 DAY CHALLENGE!

Y	1	2	3	4	5

WORK UNTIL YOUR IDOLS WANT TO COPY YOU

SIMON STEPSYS

Stay FOCUSED! Reach out in at least 3–5 ways
DAILY, complete the boxes below and put a TICK in
the circle when you've done your actions for the day!

90 DAY CHALLENGE!

1	**2**	**3**	**4**	**5**

NEVER TAKE ADVICE FROM SOMEONE WHO ISN'T WHERE YOU WANT TO BE

SIMON STEPSYS

Stay FOCUSED! Reach out in at least 3–5 ways
DAILY, complete the boxes below and put a TICK in
the circle when you've done your actions for the day!

90 DAY CHALLENGE!

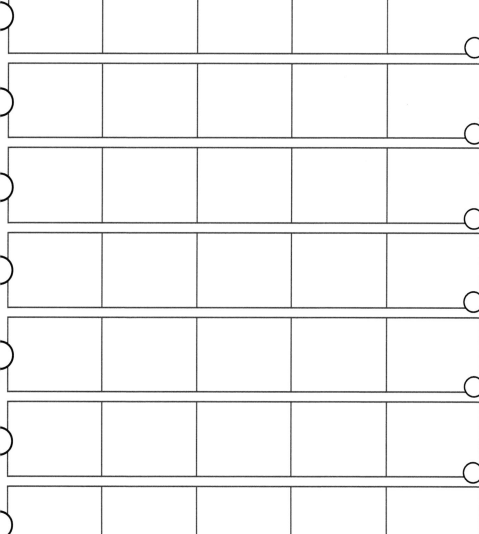

ACTION IS THE FOUNDATIONAL KEY TO ALL SUCCESS

SIMON STEPSYS

Stay FOCUSED! Reach out in at least 3–5 ways DAILY, complete the boxes below and put a TICK in the circle when you've done your actions for the day!

90 DAY CHALLENGE!

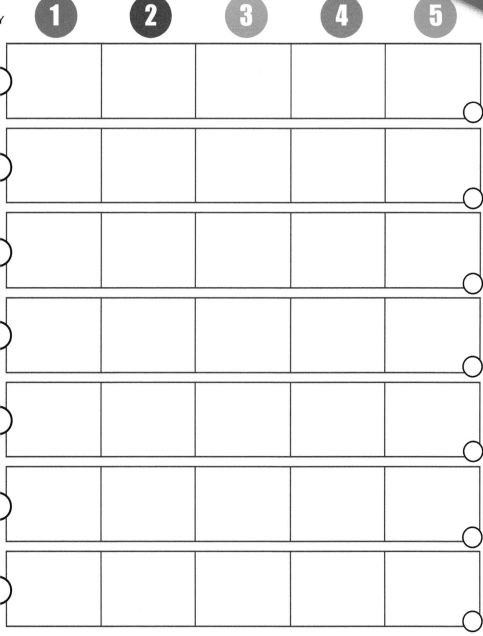

DO SOMETHING EVERY DAY THAT BRINGS YOU CLOSER TO YOUR GOALS

SIMON STEPSYS

Stay FOCUSED! Reach out in at least 3–5 ways DAILY, complete the boxes below and put a TICK in the circle when you've done your actions for the day!

90 DAY CHALLENGE!

Y	1	2	3	4	5

SUMMARY

End on a High

Want SUCCESS?

You MUST be the 3 Cs: Coachable, Committed and Consistent.

Coachable. I'm coaching you to take The 90 Day Challenge and you don't do it. You're simply not coachable.

Committed. There's an event going on in your town which provides training about your business, and you're not there – but people have flown in from another country to attend. Who is committed?

Consistent. You read this book and go flat-out for 30 days running, most probably fuelled by adrenaline and excitement. But then the next month you do nothing. There's no consistency. You have to be consistent each and *every* day.

These three attitudes are the difference between the 1% who succeed and EVERYONE else. The 1% consistently focus on The 90 Day Challenge, and they teach their teams to do the same. In fact, they finish it and start again. And that's what I want YOU to do.

If you've started the plan, missed a day, started again and then missed a few more days, you need to go back and re-read the Chapter on Discovering Your Why. It's likely that if you're not completing your 90 Days, your 'why' is not clear and your goals

Ask yourself this question at the end of every day: *'Would you employ yourself based on what you've done today?'*

If the answer is 'No', then go and get a job!

This may seem harsh but the bottom line is: this is business and it's not for everyone.

Some people are just not cut out for it.

I believe if you are the 3Cs, then you can be.

Ultimately it's all about the mindset.

If you answered 'Yes', CONGRATULATIONS!

Keep coaching others to success, and stay CONSISTENT.

aren't important enough to you. Go and look over these pages again and really dig deep. Dig until you understand what is going to truly motivate you. Once you've learned what that is, start again. When your 'why' is clear and your goals are inspiring, nothing will stop you.

Remember, I started with nothing. I used to brush the streets for a living. And now I'm an Internet Millionaire making millions of dollars, inspiring and mentoring others. I feel good when I help other people. This is my 'why'. It's what drives me each and every day.

What do you truly desire? Do you *really* want that Bentley or dream home? The freedom to live each day as you choose?

What is your goal for today, for this week? What is your goal for the next year, two years, five years and ten years? What are your daily actions to get there? The answer is easy: they are listed here! These 3–5 daily actons will help you to create the lifestyle you want. They will help you to achieve your dreams and more.

If I can do it, you can do it too. Delete the 'wussy' in you. Delete the excuses in you. Become a strong leader, and inspire others to success along the way.

Find your purpose in life, and follow your dreams.

Thank you for reading, God bless each and every one of you.

Congratulations! You did it!

You deserve a pat on the back. Great work. You completed The 90 Day Challenge. How do you feel about that?

The key now is to re-order yourself a new copy of this book, as well as multiple copies for your new team members. Coach and mentor your teams to follow the plan. This is a low-cost, low-maintenance way to blow your income out of the water!

Plus, you'll be re-reading all of the content, and therefore you'll be reminding yourself how powerful it is. I recommend you do this annually. And get all of your team to do the same.

Get multiple copies and get your team to do the same. Give copies away to new team members as a bonus for joining your business and getting started.

Think about it: if you have 10+ copies of this book and you hand them out to your team, they will be working The 90 Day Challenge and they will be accountable and will be showing you what they're doing daily.

You'll be able to coach them and offer them tips and guidance if they need it. Those with big teams, I recommend that you invest in 100+ copies.

Order your copies here:

The90DayChallenge.biz

This will continue to drive and explode your business.

Remember: consistency is key! I wish you every success in all you do.

DREAM AND DWELL ON YOUR IDEAL LIFE. FOCUS ON IT UNTIL YOU KNOW EXACTLY WHAT IT LOOKS LIKE. THEN WAKE UP AND DO AT LEAST THREE TO FIVE ACTIONS EVERY DAY TO MAKE IT A REALITY!

ALL OUT
MASSIVE ACTION PLAN

Are you ready for the next level?!!

We've all heard the advice that 10,000 steps per day is a great goal to aim for if you're looking to improve your physical health and fitness levels. For someone who does little or even no exercise each day, walking the equivalent of four miles is going to make a huge difference to how they look and feel. This advice works for the general population, those who work in offices or lead sedentary lives.

However, for a marathon runner, following this advice would not work, because it would reduce their activity levels and actually make them less fit.

The same principle applies to The 90 Day Challenge. The guidance contained within this book is aimed at getting those of you who are new (or relatively new) to Direct Sales up to a level of activity that will help you to grow your business. It's for the people who know they need to be doing more but are not sure what exactly to do. But there's a whole new level, if you're ready to go there.

Top marketers are operating at way more than 3–5 tasks per

day. In fact, it's more like 30! These people are relentless; they're focused and they can be out there non-stop promoting their business. They know that within just one hour they can reach out and build their business in a variety of ways.

I'm inviting you to live like a Top Marketer for the day and follow my All Out Massive Action Plan. For those of you who are already full time within Direct Sales, you absolutely have the time and ability to achieve 30 actions in one day. I know this because I do!

The All Out Massive Action Plan is for those of you that are highly, HIGHLY driven and ambitious. Is that you? I'm pretty certain that if you're reading this, then the answer to that question is YES.

The page that follows shows a guide and a suggestion for what an All Out Massive Action Plan can look like with a completed Action Tracker for just one day. Immediately after the completed example, you'll see that I've provided you with additional trackers, with space for you to record up to 30 actions. If you only have time to do this once or twice a week and the rest of the time you're reaching out in 3 to 5 ways, you'll still see a HUGE increase in growth.

Go for it – think big, aim big and be like the WINNERS in life.

LL OUT MASSIVE ACTION PLAN

...ail list ...ice daily ...orning & ...rly evening	Youtube video	Facebook Video	Facebook Live video	Speak to at least one new prospect
...photos to ...stagram ...th 10 ...ferent #tags	Video to Instagram # 10 different ways	Post in 20 FB groups spread across the day	Skype in 10 Skype targeted groups daily	Direct message 5 contacts in Whatsapp
...ivect ...essage ...contacts ...Linked In	Text your contacts at least 5-30 daily	Direct message 20 facebook friends	Direct message 20 prospects who are actively posting in your groups	leave at least 5 comments on target market posts on FBook
...eet 5 ...mes in ...e day. ...read it out	leave 5 comments on target market Youtube videos	place 1 new Ad on Craiglist	place 1 new Ad on Clixsense	place 1 new Ad on Neobux
...erse Email ...marketers ...no email ...a	place comment on highly targeted blog	place offline Ads in classified paper	Put out 30 drop cards	Write 500 word Blog Post
...ost ...ontent ...Tumblr	Post content on Pinterest	Book new Solo Ad on... SoloAds Guru. com	place new Ad in traffic exchange	place Ad on eBay or similar that allow Ads

ALL OUT MASSIVE ACTION PLAN

ALL OUT MASSIVE ACTION PLAN

Last but not least...

Bonus pages:

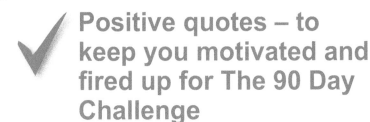

✓ **Positive quotes – to keep you motivated and fired up for The 90 Day Challenge**

✓ **Notes pages – for you to write down your goals, ideas, To-Do lists and more**

If you aren't doing what you love, you're wasting your time.

Don't watch the clock. Do what it does: keep going!

You can have results or excuses, but not both.

Don't just meet your goals, destroy them!

The only way you'll see results is if you stay consistent.

Just the fact that you're thinking about it – whether it's positive or negative – you're calling it forth into being.

Massive Action = Massive Results!!! Little action = little results (if any!!!!) Truth!

A genius spends an average 12–15 hours a day on his or her craft.

You will always get what you believe. Always!

If you walk outside and people are not asking for your autograph, it's a sign you need to work harder!

Energy flows where attention goes.

Every rejection is pushing you closer to your destination.

Ask yourself if what you're doing today is getting you closer to where you want to be tomorrow.

You are today where your thoughts have brought you; you will be tomorrow where your thoughts take you...

One word separates winners from failures: consistency.

If you are going to doubt something, doubt your limits!

Always act like you already have it!

Forget the past, focus on the future!

Think MASSIVE, dream MASSIVE, believe MASSIVE, act MASSIVE and the results will be MASSIVE!

While you're waiting, somebody else is doing it.

Be obsessed, or be average.

Every dollar I spend comes back to me tenfold!

Believe you can and you're halfway there.

A heart on fire with excitement and passion has a HUGE magnetic power.

Listen to the advice from the one who's already achieved your goal.

The fearless ones make the most money.

Your will to change should be greater than your will to remain the same.

Pain is temporary. Quitting lasts forever.

Consistency doesn't just make you rich; it makes you wealthy.

Energy and persistence conquer all things. Keep thinking positively... trust me.

When you focus on what you want, everything else falls away.

We must all suffer from one of two pains: the pain of discipline or the pain of regret. The difference is that discipline weighs ounces, while regret weighs tonnes.

Begin while others are making excuses. Work while others are wishing. Persist while others are quitting.

Staying consistent gets you to the top!

Smart people never move from the basics!!! Never!!!

Two secrets to success:
1. Get started   2. Don't quit!!!

Don't hesitate! Waiting costs you money! Always remember that money loves speed!

There is no passion to be found playing small, so THINK BIG!

The more thankful you are, the more you attract things to be thankful for.

Never be satisfied. Always strive to improve no matter how good you think you are!!!

Study the greats and become greater.

Your beliefs are a magnet that create your reality!

Hold the vision, trust the process!

Too many people FOCUS on wanting quality rather than BEING quality FIRST! Like ATTRACTS like! BE it; then and ONLY then you will attract it!

10 years from now, your kids will be eating or starving as a result of the decisions you have made today!

Be mindful of your self-talk. It's a conversation with the universe.

It's not about the money or connections. It's the willingness to outwork and outlearn everyone when it comes to your business!

Winning is average. D O M I N A T E!

Stop saying 'I want', start saying 'I have' and 'I am' !!!! #lawofattraction

We are not given a good life or a bad life. We are given a life. It's up to us to make it good or bad or great! (Make it great!)

Every second is a chance to turn your life around.

Work ethic is a talent itself!

Who wants to be a Millionaire?
STOP thinking about it. STOP dreaming about it. DO something about it...Take massive daily action! Just do it!

Work so hard that one day your signature will be called an autograph!

If you become very successful, become a great leader or win the lottery, be prepared to lose some friends and family members.

Those who are successful overcome their fears and take action. Those who aren't submit to their fears and live with regrets.

277

Be fearless!

Have a vision!

Believe in yourself!

Always hustle

Stay focused!

Get out there!

Get motivated!

Get inspired!

Use these pages to note your ideas, inspirations, goals, dreams, affirmations, desires and wants in life, income targets, and To-Do lists… DARE TO DREAM!

....
....
....
....
....
....
....
....
....
....
....
....
....
....
....
....
....
....
....
....
....
....
....
....